**MathScape™**

Seeing and Thinking
**Mathematically**

The **McGraw·Hill** Companies

Send all inquiries to:
Glencoe/McGraw-Hill
8787 Orion Place
Columbus, OH 43240-4027

ISBN: 0-07-866823-9

5 6 079 08

**Glencoe**

New York, New York
Columbus, Ohio
Chicago, Illinois
Peoria, Illinois
Woodland Hills, California

# MATHEMATICS *of* MOTION

## DISTANCE, SPEED, AND TIME

## Education Development Center, Inc.

**Curriculum Developers for**
*Mathematics of Motion*
Glenn Kleiman, Rosemary Caddy, Malcolm Swan, Hugh Burkhardt, Shelley Isaacson, Robert Bates

**EDC Project Director**
Glenn M. Kleiman

**EDC Core Staff**
Amy Brodesky, Rebecca Brown, Dan Brutlag, Emily Fagan, Kristen Herbert, Shelley Isaacson, Susan Janssen, Kathryn Rasala, Stacy Shorr, Yael Sucher, Andrea Tench, Dan Tobin, Karen Zweig

**Other EDC Contributors**
Al Cuoco, E. Paul Goldenberg, Marlene Kliman, Leigh Peake, Sue Rasala, Faye Ruopp, Kimberly Smart, Ellen Smith, Marianne Thompson, Albertha Walley, Muffie Wiebe

**Additional Contributors**
Robert Bates, George Brackett, Stacie Cassat, Daniel Pead, Michael Peller, Richard Phillips, Diane Surati

**Project Collaborators & Consultants**
EdMath, Victoria, Australia: Charles Lovitt, Doug Clarke, Ian Lowe

Shell Centre for Mathematical Education, University of Nottingham, England: Hugh Burkhardt, Rosemary Caddy, Malcolm Swan

Inverness Research Associates, Inverness, CA: Barbara Heenan, Mark St. John

Brookline Public Schools, Brookline, MA: Robert Bates

# ACKNOWLEDGMENTS

 ## MathScape Background

The STM project built upon EDC's 40-year history of developing educational materials, including PSSC Physics, ESS Science, The Infinity Factory television series, Insights Science, The Geometric Supposer software series, My Travels with Gulliver, and many other curriculum, software, and video products.

This unit is one of a series of twenty-one MathScape: Seeing and Thinking Mathematically units designed to fully address current standards and recommendations for teaching middle school mathematics. The Seeing and Thinking Mathematically project involved international collaboration with:

- The Shell Centre for Mathematical Education at the University of Nottingham, England, whose contributions built upon many years of research and development underlying materials such as The Language of Functions and Graphs.

- EdMath of Victoria, Australia, whose staff built upon years of research and development producing materials such as the Mathematics Curriculum and Teaching Program (MCTP) materials.

- Inverness Research Associates of California provided consulting on the design of the research processes used in the project and conducted research for several of the units.

The Seeing and Thinking Mathematically project incorporated many formative research activities to assist the developers in designing materials that are mathematically clear and pedagogically effective with diverse populations of students. These activities included summer institutes with middle school teachers, consultations with experts on teaching mathematics to students from different cultural and linguistic backgrounds, reviews of the research on children's learning of mathematics, input from many consultants and advisors, and classroom testing of activities in which the project staff and teachers worked closely together. These research activities helped to define the design principles used throughout the curriculum.

Building from the design principles, initial versions of each unit were then carefully tested in a variety of classrooms, ensuring feedback from multiple teachers and diverse groups of students. Project researchers conducted weekly classroom observations and teacher interviews. Student work was collected and analyzed to evaluate the lessons and identify common student misconceptions. The project researchers and curriculum developers used this extensive field test data to revise and improve the units. The field test teachers' classroom experiences and suggestions were also incorporated into the final units in the form of "From the Classroom" notes and "A Teacher Reflects."

MathScape: Seeing and Thinking Mathematically was developed by the Seeing and Thinking Mathematically project (STM), based at Education Development Center, Inc. (EDC), a nonprofit educational research and development organization in Newton, MA. The STM project was supported, in part, by the National Science Foundation Grant No. 9054677. Opinions expressed are those of the authors and not necessarily those of the Foundation.

## Field Test Teachers

*We wish to extend special thanks to the following teachers and their students for their roles in field testing and reviewing units developed by EDC.*

**ARLINGTON, MA**
Carol Martignette Boswell
Steve Porretta

**BELMONT, MA**
Tony Guarante
Heidi Johnson

**BOSTON, MA**
Patricia Jorsling
George Perry
Elizabeth Prieto
Bill Rudder

**BROOKLINE, MA**
Robert Bates
Frank Cabezas
Carolyn Connolly
Arlene Geller-Petrini
Sandra Hegsted
Oakley Hoerth
Judy McCarthy
Carol Mellet
Fran Ostrander
Barbara Scotto
Rhonda Weinstein

Debbie Winkler
Deanna Wong

**CAMBRIDGE, MA**
Mary Lou Mehring
Jennie Schmidt
Jesse Solomon

**FREMONT, CA**
Julie Dunkle

**INDIO, CA**
Lisa Sullivan

**LAKEVIEW, CA**
Jane Fesler

**MILL VALLEY, CA**
Patty Armstrong

**NEW CANAAN, CT**
Sue Kelsey
Bruce Lemoine

**NEWTON, MA**
Sonya Grodberg
David Lawrence
Mark Rubel

**SAN FRANCISCO, CA**
Ardreina Gualco
Ingrid Oyen

**SOMERVILLE, MA**
Jean Foley

**SOUTH SAN FRANCISCO, CA**
Doug Harik

**SUDBURY, MA**
Fred Gross
Sondra Hamilton
Jackie Simms

**TEMECULA, CA**
Ray Segal

**TIBURON, CA**
Julie Askeland

**WALTHAM, MA**
Amy Doherty
Diane Krueger
Pat Maloney

*We extend our appreciation to Judy Mumme and the following teachers and educators involved in the California Middle School Mathematics Renaissance Project.*

Cathy Carroll
**SAN MATEO, CA**

Deb Clay
**HUNTINGTON BEACH, CA**

Kathryn Conley
**MERCED, CA**

Joan Easterday
**SANTA ROSA, CA**

Linda Fisher
**SANTA CRUZ, CA**

Marty Hartrick
**SAN FRANCISCO, CA**

Kevin Jordan
**CARMEL, CA**

Steve Leliever
**LONG BEACH, CA**

Carole Maples
**WALNUT CREEK, CA**

Guillermo Mendieta
**AZUSA, CA**

Teferi Messert
**SACRAMENTO, CA**

Mark Rubell
**NEWTON, CA**

Charles Schindler
**RUNNING SPRINGS, CA**

Aminah Talib
**CARSON, CA**

Kevin Truitt
**LOS ANGELES, CA**

## Classroom Testing Teachers

*Our thanks to the following classroom teachers for their contributions on the MathScape units.*

Heidi Ackley
Steve Ackley
Penelope Jo Black
Bev Brockhoff
Geoff Borroughs
Linda Carmen
Janet Casagrande
Karen Chamberlin
Laura Chan
April Cherrington
Peggy Churchill
Marian Connelly
Jack Cox
Allen Craig
Barbara Creedon
Bill Cummins
Phyllis Cummins
Kathy Duane
Jennifer Dunmire
Karen Edmonds
Sara Effenbeck
Jodie Foster
John Friedrich
Barbara Gneiting
Lisa Gonzales
Ardreina Gualco
Doug Harik
Jennifer Hogerty
Lynn Hoggatt
Ron Johnson
Judy Jones
Sue Lackey
Joan LaComb
Stan Lake
Amanda LaRocca

Claudia Larson
Mona Lasley
Maria Majka
Jim McHugh
Fernando Mendez
Michael Merk
Carol Moore
John Mulkerrins
John Osness
Mary Ann Pella-Donnelly
Charles Perez
Dave Peters
Linda Peters
Lisa Phillips
Jim Pinckard
Ron Rice
Mark Ristow
Thelma Rodriguez
Ellen Ron
Emiliano Sanchez
Wes Schroeder
Janet Schwarz
Cindi Sekera
Doris Selden
Gale Sunderland
Jim Tearpak
Barbara Termaat
Brenda Walker
David Ward
Brenda Watson
Howard Web
Nancy Withers
Hanne Young

## Credits

**Teacher's Guide Credits:**
Unless otherwise indicated below, all photography by Chris Conroy.
**47B** Jerome Prevost/Getty Images; **47H** (bc) Adamski Peek/Getty Images.

**Student Guide Credits:**
Unless otherwise indicated below, all photography by Chris Conroy.
**2** Frank Herholdt/Getty Images; **3** (tr)David Madison/Getty Images, (tc b)map reproduced with permission of copyright owner, Compass Maps, Inc.; **7** NASA; **9** (bl)Froomer Pictures/Getty Images; **10** Marvin E. Newman/Getty Images; **14–15** map reproduced with permission of copyright owner, Compass Maps, Inc.; **24–25** David Madison/Getty Images; **30** Steven E. Sutton/Duomo Photography; **31** Stephen Wilkes/Getty Images; **33** Tom Raymond/Getty Images.

# TABLE OF

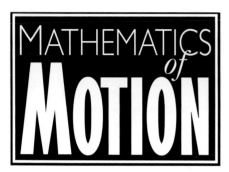

## MATHEMATICS of MOTION

### Distance, Speed, and Time

Students use mathematics to understand the fundamentals of movement. They measure, estimate, and analyze the distances, times, and speeds of their own motions. They also apply their graphing skills to the study of motion.

## PHASE ONE

### Measuring, Estimating, and Representing Motion

Students measure their own motions; estimate distance, time, and speed; describe and represent motions; and begin to explore mathematical relationships among distance, time, and speed.

## PHASE TWO

### Distance-Time Graphs

The emphasis here is on "distance-from" graphs, which show distance from a fixed reference point over time. Students learn to use such graphs to represent various motions.

# C O N T E N T S

# Additional UNIT RESOURCES

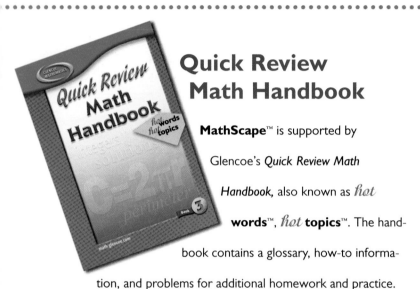

## Quick Review Math Handbook

**MathScape**™ is supported by Glencoe's *Quick Review Math Handbook,* also known as *ℏ̇ot* **words**™, *ℏ̇ot* **topics**™. The handbook contains a glossary, how-to information, and problems for additional homework and practice.

The *ℏ̇ot* **words**™ that appear on the lesson pages in the Student Guide are mathematical terms related to the lesson.

*ℏ̇ot* **topics**™ The *ℏ̇ot* **topics**™appearing in the Teacher's Guide indicate mathematical topics that are recommended for optional review and homework.

If your students do not have the *ℏ̇ot* **words**™, *ℏ̇ot* **topics**™ handbook, you can use the *ℏ̇ot* **words**™ for discussion, referencing them in any mathematical glossary or dictionary. You can use the recommended *ℏ̇ot* **topics**™ as a guide to help you organize review material.

## MathScape™ Online

Visit **www.mathscape3.com** for the following tools:

- Online Study Tools
- Technology Options
- Curriculum Links
- Teacher Reflections
- Bulletin Board

## Print Components

### Math Skills Maintenance Masters

Use the Math Skills Maintenance Masters to keep your students' basic math skills fresh. Students can review skills one at a time or in a combined format.

### Investigations for the Special Education Student in the Mathematics Classroom

Use the long-term investigations in this booklet with your special education students. Each investigation includes a list of ways in which the activities may be adapted or modified depending on the student population of the class.

| Investigation Number | Title |
|---|---|
| 7 | Vacation Getaways |
| 12 | Functions and Fitness |

## Technology Components

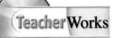

The CD-ROM includes a lesson planner and interactive Teacher's Guide, so you can customize lesson plans and reproduce classroom resources quickly and easily.

This backpack solution CD-ROM allows students instant access to the Student Guide and reproducible pages.

**ExamView Pro**

Use the networkable testmaker to:
- create multiple versions of tests,
- create modified tests for inclusion students,
- edit existing questions, and
- add your own questions.

**What's MATH Got To Do With It?** **Real-Life Math Videos**

**Level 3 Video 4** Use *Roller Coasters and Soccer* to engage your students in real-world situations involving histograms and box-and-whisker plots.

## Things You Should KNOW

The Teacher's Guide contains complete lesson plans, assessment, and reproducible pages. Look for these icons to help you make the most of the Teacher's Guide.

This icon identifies **notes** of special interest within the teaching steps. These notes often include an indication of what to expect from student writing or discussions.

This icon identifies **comments** from teachers who have used this unit in the classroom. Their experiences and practical suggestions appear in the margin of the Teacher's Guide.

A reduced version of the **Student Guide** page is shown in the Teacher's Guide for easy reference. The arrow icon is used to indicate that the notes on the Teacher's Guide page correspond directly to the Student Guide page.

# How can mathematics be used to analyze motion?

# MATHEMATICS of MOTION

## Introduction

### *How can mathematics be used to analyze motion?*

Woosh! Boing! Kerplunk! The things around us (and ourselves as well) are in nearly perpetual motion. And motion has many forms. A caterpillar inches slowly in a straight line, a CD rotates quickly while remaining at a fixed location, and a football changes speed as it accelerates along a curved trajectory.

How can we begin to understand this complex world of motion? While we may all have some intuitive understanding of motion, mathematics provides us with essential tools for analyzing movement in a wide range of contexts. In *Mathematics of Motion*, students use mathematics to examine the fundamentals of movement. They measure, estimate, and analyze the distances, times, and speeds of their own motions, such as walking or their daily trip to school. Students also learn how to use one of the most powerful mathematical tools of all (the graph) and apply it to the study of motion.

## Curriculum Links

This unit can be part of an interdisciplinary unit with physics and language arts by having students work with time-travel fiction. This unit can also be connected to physical education. The following books and materials will help students link mathematics to these topics.

### Books

*Janice VanCleave's Physics for Every Kid: 101 Easy Experiments in Motion, Heat, Light, Machines, and Sound*, by Janice VanCleave

*The Physics of Sports*, by Angelo Armenti

*Science Project About the Physics of Sports*, by Robert Gardner

*A Wrinkle in Time*, by Madeline L'Engle

### Online Research

The following words can be used as starting points for online research.
- speed
- physics
- time travel

The American Institute of Physics (AIP) publishes a free electronic newsletter for educators called *Physics Education News (PEN)*. To learn more, visit:

*www.mathscape3.com/curriculumlinks*

### PHASE**ONE**
Measuring, Estimating, and Representing Motion

In this phase, you will practice measuring motion and estimating how fast you move, how long it takes, and how far you go. Making good measurements is an important part of this beginning study of motion. You will also find new ways to represent motion in words, pictures, and diagrams.

### PHASE**TWO**
Distance-Time Graphs

First, you will walk at different speeds to collect motion data. Then you will use your data to make graphs that show how far you moved versus how long it took—distance-time graphs. You will also compare graphs with maps and stories that describe motion to find the best way to represent motion in any situation.

### PHASE**THREE**
Using Graphs to Solve Problems

For more practice graphing, you will convert a sports announcer's race commentary into a graph. You will learn about average speed and find out it might be different than speed at any particular time. You will also find out about a powerful mathematical expression for calculating distance, speed, or time of travel. A final project brings together all of your new skills in dealing with motion.

# MATHEMATICS OF MOTION
# AT A GLANCE

## PHASE ONE

### Measuring, Estimating, and Representing Motion

Phase One lays the groundwork for a mathematical study of motion by focusing on components of motion such as distance, direction, speed, and time. Students measure their own motions; estimate distance, time, and speed; describe and represent motions; and begin to explore mathematical relationships among distance, time, and speed. Students continue to study components of motion as they learn to use "snapshot sequences"—series of schematic pictures taken over a time period from a "birds-eye" view. These lessons build skills that students will later use to create, understand, and solve problems with graphs.

## PHASE TWO

### Distance-Time Graphs

The mathematical emphasis in Phase Two is on "distance-from" graphs, which show distance from the starting point over time. Students learn to use these graphs to represent various motions. Other types of distance-time graphs are also introduced, such as total distance graphs and "distance-to" graphs. These graphs represent cumulative distance and distance to a fixed reference point, respectively. Students translate among various representations of motion as they compare and contrast the information contained in graphs, maps, and verbal descriptions.

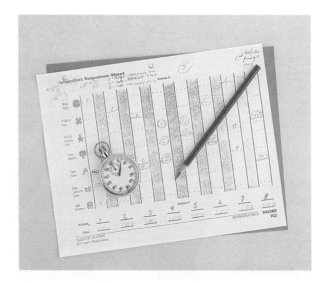

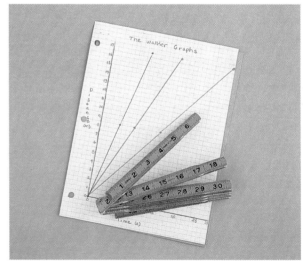

# Using Graphs to Solve Problems

In the final phase, students practice using and interpreting the three types of distance-time graphs introduced in Phase Two. Students also gain additional practice translating among distance-time graphs and verbal descriptions of the real-life situations the graphs represent. Speed-time graphs are introduced in this phase, and students learn to use them to determine average speed. Also emphasized is the equation $d = s \times t$ (and its algebraic rearrangements). Students use the equation to solve motion problems, then create graphs to check their solutions.

**MathScape:** *n:* A view of the world from a mathematical perspective.

## Math Themes

The two major math themes of this unit are **Multiple Representations** and **Proportional Reasoning.**

Students begin by representing components of motion as numbers that are obtained by measurement—measures of distance, time, and speed. Students then develop ways to represent trips visually (with maps or diagrams) and with verbal descriptions. They then explore using "snapshot sequences," which show the positions of people and objects at fixed time intervals. Snapshot diagrams provide a conceptual bridge between actual motions and distance-time graphs.

Students learn to use graphs to represent distance from a starting point, total distance traveled, and speed, as well as other changes over time. They also translate among different types of graphs and between graphs and other representations, including stories, pictures, and tables. For example, in several activities, students create stories to go with graphs and graphs to go with stories.

Throughout the unit, students use linear units (such as meters and miles) to measure distances. Students also work with speed units such as meters per second. Measuring speed requires proportional reasoning, since speed measurements are ratios of a distance and time measure. Students also use proportions to solve a variety of problems involving distances, times, and speeds, such as comparing the average speeds of runners in races of different distances.

## Math Processes

Throughout this unit, students engage in the processes of using mathematics to describe, analyze, and test predictions about motion in their world. In doing so, students learn mathematical modeling that can be a basis for many applications of mathematics in science and engineering.

When students use numbers, tables, graphs, or equations to represent how something moves, they are describing movement mathematically. They can then further analyze the motion with mathematical techniques. For example, students learn that if you know the distance someone traveled and the time they took, you can figure out the average speed with the formula speed = distance ÷ time. They also learn that if you record two different motions on a distance-time graph you can compare and contrast the motions. You can determine which mover was going faster at different times, whether the movers were moving in the same or opposite directions, and whether one or both stopped for some time period, for example.

Predictions can be made about future motion from an observed pattern of motion in the present. Mathematical tools and techniques can test the accuracy of these predictions.

These processes allow students to model the physical world and thus find out more than is directly observable—to go beyond what meets the eye in understanding the physical world.

## Math Strands

*Mathematics of Motion* integrates content from three of the major content strands: Measurement, Number and Operations, and Algebra.

Throughout the unit, students measure, estimate, and calculate distance, time, and speed. This helps them to determine measurement units (e.g., whether inches or miles are appropriate), to use both the U.S. standard and metric systems, and to find ways to convert among units within a system (e.g., to compare the speeds of runners in races of 100 meters and 5 kilometers). Students also develop techniques of computing distance, time, or speed when the other two measures are known, and they learn the basic set of equations connecting distance ($d$), speed ($s$), and time ($t$): $d = s \times t$; $s = \frac{d}{t}$; $t = \frac{d}{s}$. Students also learn to find the average speed over an interval.

The unit incorporates extensive work with coordinate graphing, including making graphs that show distance from a fixed point, total distance traveled, and speed over time. By relating different graphs to each other, to actual physical motions, to verbal descriptions of situations, and to other types of visual representations (maps, series of snapshots), students gain a clear understanding of the components of a motion (distance, speed, time, direction) and how they can be described, represented, and analyzed.

# PRE-ASSESSMENT

## PREREQUISITES

It is helpful if students enter this unit with some experience in the following skills:

- ability to make linear measurements using common measuring instruments

- understanding of U.S. standard and metric units, including inches, feet, yards, miles, centimeters, meters, and kilometers

- ability to determine distance from a map

- working with definitions of the terms *average* and *estimate*

If your students need preliminary work with these skills, you may want to review:

### hot words

- distance
- average

### hot topics

- Systems of Measurement
- Length and Distance

Have students review the unit overview on pages 46–47 in the Student Guide.

The following question is posed on page 46 of the *Mathematics of Motion* Student Guide: How can mathematics be used to analyze motion?

This question is investigated in the following pre-assessment activity, generating class discussion and individual work that helps reveal what students know about measurement, and how motion can be represented visually and mathematically.

## Materials

**Per group:**
- meterstick or yardstick
- stopwatch
- masking tape or chalk

## Opening Discussion

Help students begin to analyze motion by naming some of its features (such as speed, distance traveled, time spent) and how these features can be measured. The following questions can help guide the discussion.

- Is motion a kind of change over time? If so, what is changing?
- If you want to measure motion, what are some kinds of measurements you should make?
- What are some units of measurement you can use to measure motion?

## Prerequisite Check

Have students work in pairs. Each student should choose three different objects and estimate the length of each. Each item should be estimated in different units. Students should write down their objects and estimates, then trade lists with their partners. Partners measure the items and compare estimates to actual measurements.

## Performance Task

In this activity, students work in teams of four to hold races. The distance of the race could be the length of the classroom, its perimeter, or a set distance outside the classroom.

One member of each team should be the timer and recorder of distance, time, and speed. The other three perform the race. The rule is that the racers must stay in physical contact, but not use their hands to stay in touch.

After the race, students should cooperatively find a way to represent their motion visually. There should be three winning teams: one with the fastest average speed over all three trials, one with the fastest speed over one trial, and one team with the best visual representation of their motion.

Ask students to write in response to the question: How can math be used to analyze speed, direction, and other features of motion?

See Pre-assessment, page A4, for assessment information and sample student work.

# PLANNING AND PACING

Typically this unit takes approximately 24 class periods, each lasting 45 minutes.

| Unit Resource Manager | | | | |
|---|---|---|---|---|
| Lesson | Pacing (days) | Reproducibles | Materials (per student) | Materials (per group or class) |
| Pre-Assessment | 1 | R6 | | meterstick or yardstick<br>timer that shows seconds<br>masking tape or chalk |
| Lesson 1 | 2 | | | measuring tape, yardstick,<br>or meterstick<br>timer that shows<br>seconds<br>chalk or masking tape<br>markers or colored<br>pencils* |
| Lesson 2 | 2 | | | measuring tape, yardstick,<br>or meterstick<br>timer that shows<br>seconds<br>chalk or masking tape<br>markers or colored<br>pencils* |
| Lesson 3 | 1 | R7, R8, R10 | | |
| Lesson 4 | 2 | R8, R9, R11, R2*,<br>R5* | | |
| Lesson 5 | 2 | R12, R13 | snapshot sequence records<br>from Lessons 3 and 4 | |
| Lesson 6 | 1 | R13, R14 | | |
| Lesson 7 | 2 | | | |
| Lesson 8 | 2 | R3*, R5* | | |
| Lesson 9 | 2 | R13, R15 | | |
| Lesson 10 | 2 | R13 | | |
| Lesson 11 | 2 | R13, R16 | | |
| Lesson 12 | 2 | R4*, R5* | | See page 69B. |
| Post-Assessment | 1 | | | |

*Optional items: R2—Skill Quiz 1, R3—Skill Quiz 2, R4—Skill Quiz 3, R5—Student Assessment Criteria 1, 2, and 3

*I had very limited time for the unit, so I omitted the lessons that focused on speed-time graphs. That way my students had ample time to thoroughly explore distance-time graphs—and therefore concentrate on developing basic graphing skills. My plan was as follows:*
*Phase One: All lessons included.*
*Phase Two: All lessons, except Lesson 8, were completed.*
*Phase Three: Only Lesson 9 was completed.*
*For assessment, the class completed Lesson 8.*
*Time: 16 class sessions*

*Because I have a computer lab available and because I found the Graph Action™ software to be a powerful way to introduce distance-time graphs, I substituted computer activities using this software for Lessons 3 and 4. I then had the students complete the snapshot sequences in Lessons 3 and 4 for homework.* □

# TECHNOLOGY OPTIONS

0100101010100101010001010110111010100111010101010101010101010101111101011010101010101010101111010110101010101010110111

**Graphing Calculator**

## Lesson **5** Distance-Time Graphs

In this phase, students investigate distance-time graphs using a Calculator-Based-Ranger (CBR) application from Texas Instruments. A CBR is an effective tool for capturing real-life motion data and presenting it in graph form. In the activity described below the CBR measures, at each point in time, how far an individual student is from the starting point as he or she moves towards the CBR sensor. This data can be presented in a graph by linking the CBR directly to a TI graphing calculator using a unit-to-unit link cable. Ideally, this activity should be projected for the entire class to observe. This is a fun, active, and engaging demonstration that triggers students to make some keen observations and conclusions about how graphs are used to describe different types of "real-life" information.

**Using the CBR** If your calculator does not already have the CBR application installed, you can download it from the TI Web site. When you attach the CBR to your graphing calculator a random graph will appear automatically such as the one seen below:

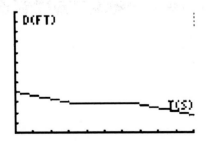

The goal of the activity is to have a student replicate this graph by walking toward the CBR sensor. The student's real time distance, at various points in time, will be recorded and graphed alongside the original graph. The student must adjust his or her position from the sensor over a given duration of time, according to the original graph. This is done by walking forward and backward at varying speeds, as well as staying still at times. It may be best to demonstrate this activity via an overhead projection so that all the students can see the graph and participate. As the student moves towards the CBR sensor, the calculator will plot his or her position.

The following graph illustrates how the screen may appear after the demonstration. The scatter plot is the student's distance-time graph.

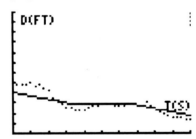

After students complete the activity, you may want to ask discussion questions like the following.

- Does the student's scatter plot accurately depict the original graph? If not, where are the differences?
- Why is the student's scatter plot different at some points than the given graph?
- Did the student ever have to speed up, slow down, or stop?
- When the graph is flat, why must the person stop moving? (Distance is not changing.)

**Software**

## Lessons **5–8** Graph Action™

The Graph Action™ software, specifically designed for *Mathematics of Motion,* supports a variety of activities that enhance the lessons in Phase Two of this unit and enables students to explore the relationship between physical motions and distance-time graphs. Students can explore how to make the graph line go up and down with different degrees of steepness, how to make the graphs for two vehicles cross or move in parallel, how to create flat sections of lines, and so on. They can also use graphs of one or two cars to predict corresponding patterns of movement, and then test their predictions. Alternatively, students can create graphs that match stories given to them, or write stories that match given graphs. They can try to produce motions that will create a total distance graph that matches a given one. In any of these activities, students can use the software to explore different possibilities, test their ideas, and pose new problems for each other.

**Software**

## Lesson **12** Action Analyzer

Graph Action Plus provides further opportunities for students to use technology to explore motions and distance-time graphs. In addition to the Graph Action program described in Phase Two, this CD-ROM contains the Action Analyzer, which enables students to create graphs of motions shown in digitized movies on the computer screen. Students can use the Action Analyzer as an optional tool in their projects in Lesson 12, when they explore a motion of their choice.

For example, students might use the Action Analyzer to explore the movements involved in juggling. The student might choose to begin with a graph showing the height of the ball over time. To create the graph, the student just needs to click on the location of the ball as the movie advances frame by frame. The result will appear on the computer screen.

The graph displays the repetitive motion of the ball moving up and down. It also shows that the maximum height of the ball varies, while the minimal height is very similar each time.

Using this software, students can add additional lines showing the height of another ball and see that the graph lines are very similar but shifted over. This shows how regular and repetitive the motion of juggling needs to be. Adding another graph line that shows the height of the juggler's hand enables students to make some more discoveries. The lines on the graph now show exactly when the juggler catches and releases each ball.

A final program on the CD-ROM, Multi-Viewer, enables students to create a display showing a maximum of four windows, with a movie or graph in each one. This can be useful in developing a computer component to their project reports.

MathScape™ Online

**For additional technology activities, a link to the Texas Instrument Web site, and information about Graph Action Plus, visit:**

*www.mathscape3.com/technology*

To: Future Olympic Runners

To improve your performance, we on the coaching staff want you to learn more about motion. The more you know, the more you can track your progress. The first thing you need to do is to take accurate measurements of how far you run. You also need to find out how you can determine speed if you know your distance and time. Because you may not always be able to measure your motion, you should also be able to make accurate estimates of distance, time, and speed. We will want to discuss your training sessions, so it's important to know how to describe and represent your motion too.

### Measuring and Estimating Motions

The *Mathematics of Motion* unit helps students use mathematics to capture information about movement in the physical world and to analyze that information with mathematical tools and techniques.

Phase One begins with students measuring their own movements and trying to move in ways that match target measures (e.g., walk at exactly 1 meter per second for 10 seconds). Students also measure, estimate, and research information about the movements of people, animals, and vehicles.

Throughout the unit, students use linear units, including inches, feet, centimeters, meters, kilometers, and miles, to measure distances. They also work with units for measuring speed and rates, such as feet per second, miles per hour, and beats per minute. Understanding the meaning of *per* in units such as *miles per hour* is an important goal of the unit.

### Relating Distance, Speed, and Time

In this phase, students combine their work in measuring, estimating, and researching motions with exploration of the basic mathematical relationships among distance ($d$), time ($t$), and speed ($s$), as shown by the three equations $d = s \times t$, $s = d \div t$, and $t = d \div s$.

## Representing Motion Visually

Phase One also begins a focus, which continues throughout the unit, on visual ways of representing motion. In Lesson 1, students create their own visual representations of a trip to school or another place they go frequently. Students also write a description of the same trip.

Lessons 3 and 4 provide a bridge between physical motions and the distance-time graphs that are introduced in Phase Two. These lessons develop students' abilities to analyze and visualize motions through work with "snapshot sequences," series of schematic pictures taken at regular intervals from a "bird's-eye" view. When lined up together, the snapshot sequence pictures show the position of each person and object on the road at the time each picture was taken.

Snapshot diagrams make intuitive sense to students—they can easily imagine how the snapshots were taken and the physical movements shown by the sequence. These snapshot sequences provide a concrete way of thinking about many of the elements of distance-time graphs. For example, distance is shown on the vertical axis and time along the horizontal axis. If two objects start at the same position and one moves faster than the other, the faster object moves up more quickly, just as a steeper slope conveys a faster speed on a distance-time graph.

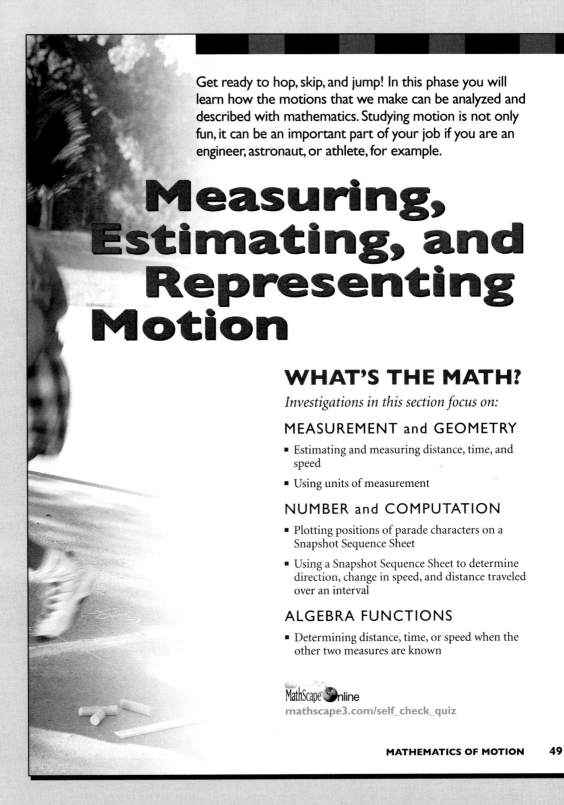

Get ready to hop, skip, and jump! In this phase you will learn how the motions that we make can be analyzed and described with mathematics. Studying motion is not only fun, it can be an important part of your job if you are an engineer, astronaut, or athlete, for example.

# Measuring, Estimating, and Representing Motion

## WHAT'S THE MATH?

*Investigations in this section focus on:*

### MEASUREMENT and GEOMETRY

- Estimating and measuring distance, time, and speed
- Using units of measurement

### NUMBER and COMPUTATION

- Plotting positions of parade characters on a Snapshot Sequence Sheet
- Using a Snapshot Sequence Sheet to determine direction, change in speed, and distance traveled over an interval

### ALGEBRA FUNCTIONS

- Determining distance, time, or speed when the other two measures are known

MathScape Online
**mathscape3.com/self_check_quiz**

# AT A GLANCE

# Moving, Measuring, and Representing

Students begin *Mathematics of Motion* with a discussion of units and then perform an activity. They move in various ways—hopping, walking, skipping—while trying to move at precise, designated speeds. To check how well they have matched their target speeds, students measure and estimate their times of travel, distances moved, and speeds. An opportunity to verbally and visually represent motion comes next, as students describe their daily trip to school then represent it with a diagram, map, drawing, or other visual means.

## Mathematical Goals

- Measure and estimate distance, time, and speed.
- Relate distance, time, and speed measures to personal experience.
- Use units of measurement.
- Describe features of motion verbally.
- Visually represent motion.

**MATERIALS**

**PER GROUP**

- measuring tape, yardstick, or meterstick
- clock, watch, stopwatch, or timer that shows seconds
- chalk or masking tape
- markers or colored pencils (optional)

**PREPARATION**

To prepare for Step 4, you may want students to take notes on their trip to school. They might note the time it takes, distance, speed, mode of transportation, and landmarks.

# Going the Distance

Students first estimate and then measure how far they go in 10 seconds when moving in different ways, such as walking quickly or walking backwards. They use this information to calculate how far they would go in longer periods of time, and how long it would take them to go 1 mile or 1 kilometer. Students then use estimates, measurements, and calculations to find the distance, time, and speed involved in going various places by various means.

## Mathematical Goals

- Measure distance, time, and speed.
- Estimate distance, time, and speed.
- Determine distance, time, or speed when the other two measures are known.

**MATERIALS**

**PER GROUP**

- measuring tape, yardstick, or meterstick
- clock, watch, stopwatch, or timer that shows seconds
- chalk or masking tape
- markers or colored pencils (optional)

**PREPARATION**

The first activity requires a space where students can walk quickly for 10 seconds. If space is not available, students can collect this data for homework.

LESSON 3

# Reporting Live from the Parade

Students read a narrative in which a photographer in a hot air balloon is taking a series of snapshots of a parade below. They are introduced to several characters in the parade. Students use the information in the narrative to construct a "snapshot sequence" that reflects the distance traveled and the direction of the various parade characters over time. The snapshot sequence helps students visualize and analyze motions and prepares them for later work with distance-time graphs.

## Mathematical Goals

- Identify the following aspects of motions:

  time interval

  position at a given time

  relative speed of movement ("faster," "slower")

  actual speed (meters per second)

- Interpret and use parts of snapshot sequences that resemble features of graphs, including scales of axes and coordinate position.

**MATERIALS**

**PER STUDENT**

- Reproducible R8 (two copies)
- Reproducible R10

**PER GROUP**

- Reproducible R7

LESSON 4

# The Parade Continues

Students are given another narrative and set of field notes describing the parade. Clouds block the view during several snapshots, so some data is missing. Students use the given information to figure out the positions of the characters in the missing snapshots. Students also create snapshots as they would look if a picture were taken every 1 second, instead of every 5 seconds.

Next, students are given a completed snapshot sequence, but with the context, characters, roadside objects, and time intervals left for them to define. They create their own stories or field notes to go with this snapshot sequence.

## Mathematical Goals

- Identify the following aspects of motions (in addition to those in Lesson 3):

  direction

  change in speed

  distance traveled

- Interpolate intervening values.

**MATERIALS**

**PER STUDENT**

- Reproducible R8 (two copies)
- Reproducibles R9 and R11

# 1

**Investigating Rates of Motion**

*This activity got students involved in measuring time and distance carefully and in using feet-per-second and meters-per-second. They found it surprising how difficult it was to estimate the speed at which they were moving—so did I and other teachers when we tried some of the challenges ourselves.* ☐

*We held the discussion in a whole-class format. It was great for brainstorming and establishing an understanding of distance and speed.* ☐

# Moving, Measuring, and Representing

Have students review the phase overview on pages 48–49 in the Student Guide.

## 1 Discussing Motion and How to Measure It

Before the investigation, have students brainstorm to describe objects that move in different ways. Next, ask what units of measurement are used for each kind of motion. (Possible answers: the fast, constant-speed, straight-line motion of a car on a freeway—units are kilometers per hour; the back-and-forth motion of a pendulum—units are cycles per minute; the turning motion of a CD—units are rotations per second.)

These follow-up discussion questions focus on units of measurement.

- What do the units of measurement on the list have in common? (Answer: The units specify some distance moved or action taken per unit of time.)

- What does *per* stand for? (Answer: *Per* means "for each.")

 Early in this lesson, speed is used in the everyday sense of rate—how quickly something happens. Later, students will refine their thinking and define speed in the strict sense used in physics—as distance moved per unit of time.

## 2 Moving at Precise Speeds

*student page*

Students can perform the activities inside the classroom. However, if you are able to let students work in a hallway, playground, gymnasium, or other large area, they can move (walk, run, hop, etc.) with higher speeds and experiment with longer distances. If students are in a space larger than the classroom, you might have them also collect data for the first activity of Lesson 2. The following discussion questions will help students analyze their own problem-solving methods.

- Which was the easiest motion to measure? Why?

- Which was the hardest motion to measure? Why?

- How did you use distance and time measurements to determine speed?

You may wish to have partners trade papers to discuss their examples. A chart featuring responses from each pair can be compiled on the blackboard.

This activity provides kinesthetic and visual experiences to help students develop an understanding of three key aspects of motion—speed, distance, and time (duration).

Student work shown on the following pages is provided as a guide only.

# homework options

**LESSON HOMEWORK**

*Page 78*

## *hot* topics

- *Systems of Measurement (8•1)*
  *Exercises 1–10*

---

Move at Precise Speeds

When I was the mover, I tried crawling, jumping, and skipping. I predicted I could crawl 1 meter in 10 seconds, jump up one time in 1 second and skip 10 meters in 10 seconds or 1 meter/second. When we measured, we found I actually crawled 97 feet in 10 second and skipped 20 meters in 10 seconds so my ... jumped three times in 1 ... speed for skipping was 2 meters per second.

Describe Motions with Precise Speeds
5 feet per second – running baby
3 meters per second – running human
50 meters per hour – bug walking
10 miles per hour – dog running
50 miles per hour – car in slow lane
1200 miles per hour – airplane

---

# 1 Moving, Measuring, and Representing

**INVESTIGATING RATES OF MOTION**

**Fast or slow, up or down, turning, twisting, or straight— there are many kinds of motion.** You will move your body in different ways, estimate and measure speed and distance, and use different methods to represent motion.

## Move at Precise Speeds

**How closely can you estimate the speed of motion?**

In the following activities, work with your partner. Take turns being the mover and the measurer.

**1** The mover tries to move at exactly the speed given in the List of Motions without looking at a clock or watch. The measurer measures, times, and checks the mover.

**2** Make up new motions at precise speeds. Choose what the mover should do and how fast the mover should go. Record what motions you tried and what happened.

**3** Write a description of something that might move at each of the following speeds:

a. 5 feet per second
b. 3 meters per second
c. 50 meters per hour
d. 10 miles per hour
e. 50 miles per hour
f. 1,200 miles per hour

### List of Motions

Tap a pencil at exactly 1 tap per second for 10 seconds.

Turn the pages of a book at exactly 2 pages per second for 10 seconds.

Move at a speed of exactly 1 foot per second for 30 seconds.

Walk from your seat to the classroom door at a speed of 2 feet per second.

Tap a pencil every 5 seconds for 1 minute.

Turn the pages of a book at exactly 1 page per second for 20 seconds.

Move at a speed of exactly 1 meter per second for 10 seconds.

Walk the length of the classroom in exactly 15 seconds. What was your speed?

50   **MATHEMATICS OF MOTION • LESSON 1**

**MATHEMATICS OF MOTION • LESSON 1**   **50**

*Most of my students created maps to visually represent their trips to school. Generally, they showed distance by some sort of key, using different colors to show different distances. Some marked times along the way, but most did not. One had a very different representation—a series of still pictures of places along the way, without showing how he got from place to place. To my surprise, only a few tried to draw maps to scale, and no one drew a graph. □*

*I was glad I decided to try this part of the lesson. The students got very engaged in creating their visual representations and stories. Also, it led to a good discussion about different ways to represent distance, time, direction, and speed. After my students drafted written and visual descriptions of their trips to school, I had them swap their work with a partner. I gave each student a feedback form to evaluate their partner's work. The feedback form asked students to state the main strengths and weaknesses of their partner's representations. Students' used the feedback to improve their work. □*

*student page*

## 3 Representing Your Trip to School

Students may use a variety of written formats to describe their trip to school. Stories, descriptive paragraphs, and detailed notes are some possibilities. If students live right next to the school, they can describe how they get to a park, store, or a friend's house.

## 4 Comparing Representations of Motion

Before having a class discussion, you may wish to have each student present his or her work to the class. Alternatively, representations could be posted. The following questions focus on the key mathematical question of the investigation: What information is shown by different representations of the trip to school?

- What kinds of information about the trip do drawings show? What kinds of information do drawings not show? (Possible answer: Drawings show landmarks and direction of travel but not speed or time elapsed.)

- What kinds of information about the trip do maps show? What don't maps show? (Possible answer: Maps show distance and direction but not time or speed.)

- What kinds of information about the trip do graphs show? What don't graphs show? (Possible answer: Graphs show distance, time, and speed of travel, but landmarks are not shown.)

# what to look for

**DOES STUDENT WORK SHOW:**

- *ability to measure correctly, including correct use of units?*
- *reasonable estimates of time, distance, and speed?*
- *representations of motion that include important features of motion such as distance traveled, direction, or landmarks*

See *Mathematics of Motion* Assessment page A5 for assessment information.

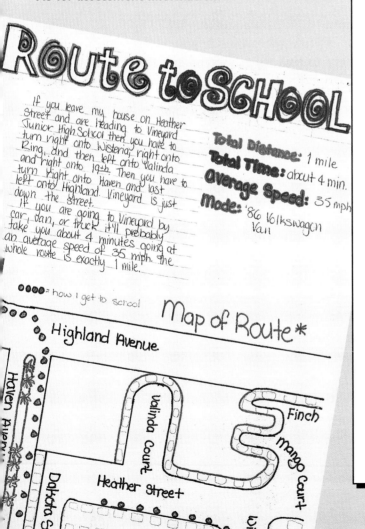

**Route to SCHOOL**

If you leave my house on Heather Street and are heading to Vineyard Junior High School then you have to turn right onto Wisteria, right onto Ring, and then left onto Valinda and right onto 19th. Then you have to turn right onto Haven and last left onto Highland. Vineyard is just down the street.
If you are going to Vineyard by car, van, or truck it'll probably take you about 4 minutes going at an average speed of 35 mph. The whole route is exactly 1 mile.

**Total Distance:** 1 mile
**Total Time:** about 4 min.
**Average Speed:** 35 mph
**Mode:** '86 Volkswagen Van

●●●● = how I get to school

**Map of Route ***

Highland Avenue

Finch

Valinda Court

Mango Court

Heather Street

Haven Avenue

Dakota Street

Wisteria

## Represent Your Trip to School

If you need to explain how something moves, there are different kinds of representations to choose from. For example, consider how you can represent the motion of your daily trip to school.

> **How can words and visual images be used to represent motion?**

**1** Describe how you get to school in writing. You can use a story, a set of directions, or any other way to describe your trip in words. Make sure someone could tell from your description whether you walk or ride to school, how long it takes you to get there, and how far and how fast you travel.

**2** Show your trip to school visually. You can use a map, a diagram, a graph, pictures, or any other kind of visual representation.

**3** Use the list Things to Know About Your Trip to answer the following two questions.

  **a.** What could someone learn about your trip by reading your description of it?

  **b.** What could they learn by looking at your visual representation?

### Things to Know About Your Trip

- Each turn that you make along the way
- The names of the streets
- The mode of transportation (walk, bicycle, bus, car, train)
- The distance of the entire trip
- The distance of each part of the trip
- The time of the entire trip
- The time of each part of the trip
- Whether you go with anyone else
- The speed you travel for each part of the trip

**hot words** | estimate

**Homework**
page 78

# 2

## Estimating, Measuring, and Calculating Distance

*Students used different strategies for measuring how far they moved. Some groups used the paper metersticks I prepared. Others discovered that they could mark off longer distances, such as 3 meters, and then simply measure how far beyond these marks they moved.* ☐

*In order to arrange for a large space for this activity, I asked the gym teacher to participate. Students made their estimates in math class, and then took their measurements during gym class. This made the activity easy to manage as well as reinforced the connection between math and sports.* ☐

# Going the Distance

*student page*

## 1 Finding Out How Far

Have students work in pairs to estimate and measure how far they travel in 10 seconds when moving in different ways. Then have them use their estimates to calculate how far they would travel in various time periods and the time it would take to travel 1 mile or 1 kilometer.

Before beginning, have students practice estimating lengths with the following questions. Have volunteers measure each distance with a meterstick and report the answers to the class.

- What is the length of the blackboard?
- How far is it from the floor to ceiling?
- What is the height of the classroom door?

Pair students and move to a large space, such as a hallway, gym, or playground, where they have room to walk or hop for 10 seconds. (If no space is available on campus, students can collect their data as homework.) Allow them to work out their own ways to solve the problems. This provides a basis for understanding equations introduced later in the lesson.

 You can choose whether students should use feet and miles or meters and kilometers for this activity, or let the students decide.

## 2 Thinking About Units of Measurement

To focus on units of measurement and how to convert between units, have students write responses to the following questions.

- How did you decide what measurement unit to use in each column of your table? For example, did you use the same unit for distance in 1 second and distance in 1 hour?

- How did you convert between measurement units when making your calculations? For example, how did you find the number of miles or kilometers you could go in 1 hour from your measurements of 10 seconds?

## 3 Exploring the Data

The next questions addresses statistical concepts. To answer them, you will need to gather results from all the students and put their data on the blackboard.

- If we look at the data for the whole class, what is the range of distances in 1 hour for each way of moving?

- What's the class median? the class mean?

| | Estimate: Distance in 10 seconds | Measure: Distance in 10 seconds | Calculate: Distance in 1 second | Calculate: Distance in 1 minute | Calculate: Distance in 1 hour | Calculate: Time to go 1 mile or 1 km |
|---|---|---|---|---|---|---|
| Walking at your regular pace | 12 meters | 11.5 meters | 1.15 meters | 69 meters | 4140 meters | 14.5 minutes |
| Walking quickly | 20 meters | 23.5 meters | 2.35 meters | 141 meters | 8460 meters | 7.1 minutes |
| Hopping | 15 meters | 30 meters | 3 meters | 180 meters | 10800 meters | 5.56 minutes |
| Walking backwards | 8 meters | 21.5 meters | 2.15 meters | 129 meters | 7740 meters | 7.5 minutes |
| A way of moving you make up crab walk | 6 meters | 15 meters | 1.5 meters | 90 meters | 5400 meters | 11.12 minutes |

# 2 Going the Distance

ESTIMATING, MEASURING, AND CALCULATING DISTANCE

**To find out how far it is from one point to another, do you estimate the distance? measure it? calculate it?** In this lesson, you will have the chance to use all three ways of finding distance.

## Find Out How Far

When you move from here to there, how do you know how far you have gone?

**1** Copy the table Knowing the Distance in your notebook or on another sheet of paper. Without actually walking or measuring, estimate how far you will go in 10 seconds when you move each way listed in the table. Record your estimates in your table.

**2** Working with your partners, measure how far you actually go in 10 seconds for each way of moving. How do your estimates compare with your measurement results?

**3** Using the data from the second column, calculate how far you would go in 1 second, 1 minute, and 1 hour; and how long it would take you to go 1 mile or 1 kilometer.

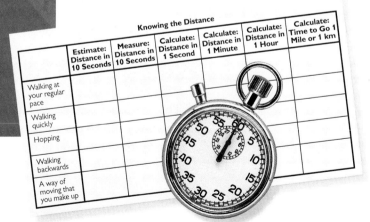

Knowing the Distance

| | Estimate: Distance in 10 Seconds | Measure: Distance in 10 Seconds | Calculate: Distance in 1 Second | Calculate: Distance in 1 Minute | Calculate: Distance in 1 Hour | Calculate: Time to Go 1 Mile or 1 km |
|---|---|---|---|---|---|---|
| Walking at your regular pace | | | | | | |
| Walking quickly | | | | | | |
| Hopping | | | | | | |
| Walking backwards | | | | | | |
| A way of moving that you make up | | | | | | |

**52** **MATHEMATICS OF MOTION** • LESSON 2

To help my students gauge distances, I pointed out that the tiles on the classroom floor are about 1 foot. Students shared examples of distances they knew, such as a football field, which is 100 yards, and the diagonal path across the school playground, which they run in gym class, which is 50 meters. □

I was struck by the different approaches my students took to this activity. Some used only examples of familiar trips. For example, Keith used examples of his daily trip to the Boys' and Girls' Club. Other students enjoyed thinking about fantasy trips, for example, to Africa by plane, to the moon by rocket, and to California by foot! □

## 4 Relating How Long? How Far? and How Fast?

*student page*

This activity involves larger scale measurements and estimate. Students relate measures of distance, time, and speed to places and motions that they know. To activate students' intuitive ideas about how speed, time, and distance relate, ask the following questions:

- If a dog runs twice as fast as you, how much farther can he run in 10 minutes? (Answer: Twice as far.)

- Suppose the movie theater is ten times as far away as the mall, but it takes just as long to get to both places. How do your speeds to each place compare? (Answer: Your speed to the theater is ten times as fast as your speed to the mall.)

Allow students to work in groups and find their own ways to determine distance, time, or speed when two of the measures are known. Some will make estimates; others may use calculations.

## 5 Explaining Your Solutions

*student page*

The writing exercise asks students to focus on how they solved distance, time, and speed problems in the table. You may want students to write their responses individually and then discuss them in small groups.

## 6 Finding an Equation for Distance, Time, and Speed

Before introducing the distance equation, ask volunteers to present any calculations they used for the table. Next, explain the equation $d = st$. Students can practice applying it with the following problems. You may also wish to have students make up problems to trade with partners.

- A car travels 30 miles per hour for 12 hours. How far does it travel? (Answer: 360 miles)

- A bug crawls uphill for 25 minutes at 0.15 mile per hour. How far does it go? (Answer: 0.0625 miles, or 330 feet)

- If you can bicycle to the mall in 20 minutes while going 11 miles per hour, how far away is the mall? (Answer: 3.67 miles)

The following examples provide practice in rearranging the equation to solve for speed or time rather than distance.

- A swimmer swims 65 meters in 7 minutes. What is her speed? (Answer: 9.29 meters per minute)

- How long does it take a ball rolling 1.75 feet each second to go the 100 yards from one goal line of a football field to the other? (Answer: 171.43 seconds, or 2.86 minutes)

- *concrete understandings of the sizes of feet, meters, kilometers, miles, and so on?*
- *ability to convert from one unit to another?*
- *accurate measurement of speed?*
- *ability to approximately determine distance, time, or speed when two of these measures are known?*

**See *Mathematics of Motion* Assessment page A5 for assessment information.**

| From | To | How? | How Far? | How Long? | How Fast! |
|------|-----|------|----------|-----------|-----------|
| your desk | classroom door | foot | about 20 feet | about 5 sec | |
| gas station | our school | foot | about 1 mile | about half an hour | 4 ft per sec |
| my house | my uncle's house | bike | about 10 miles | 30 minutes | 2 mph |
| my school | beach | bus | about 150 miles | 3 hours | $\frac{1}{3}$ mph / 50 mph |

I had to guess about the beach trip we took last year. I remember it took 3 hours to get there! I just guessed that a school bus would go 50 mph and so the trip would be about 150 miles.

## Relate How Long? How Far? and How Fast?

Copy the table Going Places in your notebook or on a sheet of paper. Include all the information already given. Then fill in the rest of your copy of the table. Each row should show places you could start from and go to, how you could get there (by foot, by bike, by bus, etc.), and the distance, time, and speed of the trip. You may have to estimate some of the information. Some of it you will find by making calculations.

**Is there a relationship between time, distance, and speed?**

| | | Going Places | | | |
|------|-----|-----------------------|----------------------|--------------------|----------------------|
| **From** | **To** | **How?** (foot, bus, etc.) | **How Far?** (distance) | **How Long?** (time) | **How Fast?** (speed) |
| your desk | classroom door | foot | | | |
| | our school | | about 1 mile | | |
| | | | | 30 minutes | |
| | | | | | 50 miles per hour |
| | | | | | |

## Explain Your Solutions

After you have completed the table, choose one distance, one time, and one speed that you were not able to measure directly. Describe in writing why you couldn't measure it directly and how you figured out the numbers you put in the table.

*hot* **words** | equation
distance

**H**omework
page 79

**Representing Motion with Picture Coordinates**

*I'm glad that I took a moment to review the time representation used in Latasha's Field Notes (e.g., "1:00:05" is "5 seconds past 1 o'clock"). Many of my students didn't recognize the representation until I compared it to the familiar "hours:minutes:seconds" display from digital stopwatches.* □

*I had my students read the narrative in groups of three with one member playing each part. This helped each student concentrate and figure out what was going on. I also had students discuss the follow-up questions in their small groups before going over them with the whole class.* □

# Reporting Live from the Parade

## 1 Setting the Scene

This activity primes students to learn about coordinate graphs in a later lesson. For the first time, they see how a system of axes can be used to describe the major elements of motion—distance, time, speed, and direction. The narrative Reporting Live from the Parade, Reproducible R7, introduces the parade context, which is used in this lesson and in Lesson 4. You may want to read the narrative aloud, or distribute copies so students can read it independently.

To check understanding, ask the following questions.

- Who is Monica Chang, and what is she doing?

- Who are JT and Latasha, and what are they doing?

- How often does JT take a photo?

 Students should save their snapshot sequences from this lesson and Lesson 4 for use in Lesson 5.

## *student page* → 2 Using Snapshots to Represent Motion

Give each student two copies of Reproducible R8, the Snapshot Sequence Sheet. One copy will be used now, and the other in Step 3. Ask students to use Latasha's Field Notes I, Reproducible R10, to determine where each parade character is at each 5-second interval and then place the character in the correct position on the sheet.

Introduce the Snapshot Sequence Sheet by discussing some of its features (e.g., each snapshot represents the same road at a different time; the snapshots are placed side by side to show the sequence; there are 5 seconds between each snapshot; the booths along the side of the road are 15 meters apart).

Check understanding of the snapshot sequence with questions such as these:

- How far is it from the gas station at Avenue A to the stop sign at Avenue B? (90 m)

- How far is it from one booth to the next? (15 m)

- How far is it from the Gas Station to the Dog Lovers' Club? from the TreeWatch booth to the Stop Sign? (15 m; 45 m)

- How much time is represented by snapshots 1–8 all together? (35 sec)

# homework options

**LESSON HOMEWORK**

*Page 80*

*hot* **topics**

- *Writing Expressions and Equations (6•1)*
  *Exercises 1–25*

## Snapshot Sequence Sheet

SNAPSHOTS 1–8

Stop
Sign

[STOP]

T-Shirt
Hut

C.O.
onicle

Watch

Avenue B

Avenue A

1       2       3       4       5       6       7       8
1:00:00  1:00:15  1:00:10  1:00:15  1:00:20  1:00:25  1:00:30  1:00:35

= rollerblader
= drummajor
= dragonfloat

---

# 3 Reporting Live from the Parade

REPRESENTING
MOTION WITH
PICTURE
COORDINATES

**Have you ever seen the film used in movie projectors?**
Each frame, or "snapshot," shows the scene at a different time. Taken together, the snapshots show action. You can use written snapshots to create a visual representation of the action at a parade.

## Use Snapshots to Represent Motion

**How can snapshots be used to show the motions of parade characters?**

When you read the handout Reporting Live from the Parade, you learned that Monica Chang is a radio reporter covering a parade. JT Diaz, the photographer, takes a snapshot every 5 seconds, capturing the changing positions of parade characters. Latasha Williams is JT's assistant. She takes detailed notes describing the scenes in JT's photos.

**1** Use the information in the handout Latasha's Field Notes I, snapshots 1–8, to complete a Snapshot Sequence Sheet. For each snapshot, fill in the snapshot number and the time.

**2** Record the position of the rollerblader, the drum major, and the dragon float when JT took snapshots 1–8. Choose a letter, symbol, or color to represent each parade character.

**54**   **MATHEMATICS OF MOTION** • LESSON 3

**MATHEMATICS OF MOTION** • LESSON 3     **54**

*The question, "Why is Lisa in such a hurry?" prompted a lot of thinking and many plausible explanations. A representative response: "I think the Dragon Float ran over the Juggler, so Lisa went running over to get a report on what happened."* ☐

*Several of my students wrote correct equations of motion, except that they didn't include conversion factors to end up with the desired units. When we reviewed the exercise, we got the chance to talk about this and practice setting up conversion factors.* ☐

## 3 Practicing Problem Solving with the Snapshots

Explain to students that they will use Latasha's Field Notes I: Film Roll 1, Snapshots 17–24, to complete their second Snapshot Sequence Sheet. You may want students to work in pairs to complete the assignment.

## 4 Discussing the Motions of Parade Characters

The following discussion questions focus on the math goals of the lesson, and refer to the snapshot sequences for snapshots 1–8 and 17–24. You may want to have students work on these questions in pairs before discussing them with the whole class, so that they can closely analyze their Snapshot Sequence Sheets.

- In the snapshot sequence for snapshots 1–8, who is traveling the fastest? (Answer: RB) the slowest? (Answer: DF) How can you tell? (Possible answer: By comparing distances traveled in a typical 5-second interval)

- How fast, in meters per second, is each character moving during the first 4 intervals? (Answers: RB = 2 m/sec; DM = 1 m/sec; DF = 0 m/sec) How can you tell? (Possible answer: Calculate speed = distance ÷ time for each character during the first 4 intervals.

- How far will each parade character move in 5 minutes, assuming that the characters continue moving at a constant rate for 5 minutes? (Answers: RB = 600 m; DM = 300 m. It is uncertain how far DF will move because its speed is not constant. Responses for L and J

based on their speeds during intervals of recorded movement: L = 900 m; J = 600 m.) How can you tell? (Answer: Use the distance equation.) How many snapshots would JT take to show the whole 5 minutes? (Answer: 60)

- What might the Dragon Float, the Juggler, and Lisa have been doing in snapshots 22–24? (Answer: They could have been enjoying the T-Shirt Hut.) Why do you think so? (Answer: They were not moving.)

## 5 Writing Equations for Motion

Students write equations to find the number of times various things happen, or the distance a parade character will travel, for any given number of minutes. Those who are not yet able to write equations can describe their rules in words. [Answers: 1. $P = 12M$, or the number of photos equals 12 times the number of minutes; 2. Since rate is 1 m/sec, $D = 60M$ meters, or the number of meters marched equals 60 times the number of minutes; 3. RB: $D = 120M$ meters; DF: $D = 60M$ meters (when moving)]

# what to look for

**DO STUDENTS' RESPONSES TO THE SNAPSHOT SEQUENCES SHOW:**

- *correct placement of characters with respect to time and position for each snapshot?*
- *recognition of the relative speeds of parade characters?*
- *correct determination of actual speed (in meters per second)?*

**See *Mathematics of Motion* Assessment page A5 for assessment information.**

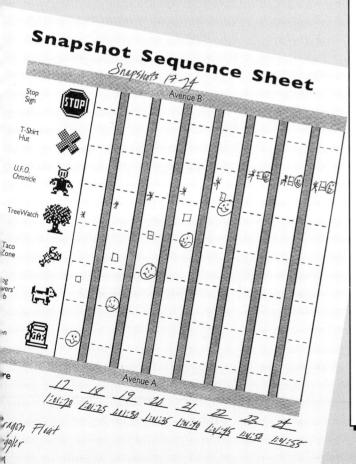

## Practice Problem Solving with the Snapshots

Read the following bulletin just in from the parade:

**Live from the Parade**

"This is Monica Chang again, from KMTH radio, bringing you more live coverage from the Main Street parade. JT has been taking pictures during our commercial break, and he tells me he's getting ready to take his 17th picture. The dragon float is still in view. We can also see a juggler on a unicycle and Lisa, a photographer friend of JT's from the newspaper. Lisa is jogging with her camera. That is unusual. I wonder why she's in such a hurry?"

- Make another visual representation of the action at the parade. This time, use the handout Latasha's Field Notes I for snapshots 17–24 and another Snapshot Sequence Sheet.

- Answer the question, "Why is Lisa in such a hurry?"

## Write Equations for Motion

Use your Snapshot Sequence Sheets to write equations describing motion at the parade.

**1** Write a rule you can use to figure out how many snapshots JT would take in any given number of minutes. Use *P* to stand for the number of snapshots, and *M* to stand for the number of minutes.

**2** Assuming the drum major moves at a constant rate, write a rule you can use to figure out how far in meters the drum major would march in a given number of minutes. Use *D* to stand for the distance in meters he marches and *M* to stand for the number of minutes.

**3** Assuming they move at constant rates, write rules to find the distance in meters the rollerblader and the dragon float move in any given number of minutes.

*hot* **words** | coordinates
equation

**H**◆**mework**

page 80

# 4
**LESSON**

## Finding Data from a Snapshot Sequence

*I made a transparency of the Snapshot Sequence Sheet and filled in the given positions of characters. After everyone had completed the activity, volunteers came up to the overhead and filled in the positions that had been obscured by clouds. It was a good way for everyone to check their work.*

*Students had two different basic approaches to finding the missing data. Most solved for the speed of each character and then plotted points in the missing snapshot frames. Some solved the problem graphically, however, drawing straight lines through the given positions and interpolating the missing points.* □

# The Parade Continues

## 1 Setting the Scene

Begin by having students read the narrative Reporting Live from the Clouds. Use the following discussion questions to check for understanding.

- What has changed since Monica's first report?

- What is unusual about the pig in the parade?

*student page*

## 2 Finding Missing Data

Give each student a copy of Latasha's Field Notes II, Reproducible R11, and a Snapshot Sequence Sheet, Reproducible R8. Then explain that they should use Latasha's Field Notes II to record the positions of the parade characters on the sheet.

Students may work individually or in pairs. For follow-up, you can ask the following questions, which should be left open-ended, allowing students to reflect on them as they complete the lesson.

- Is each character moving at a constant pace? How can you tell?

- How did you fill in the missing positions?

- What is the speed of each character?

- How can you express the direction of the pig's route?

In making snapshot sequences, students are asked to use given information (the positions of the characters at certain times) to approximate other information (the positions of the characters between those times). This is analogous to graph-making where known information on a graph is used to approximate other information, such as data points between plotted points.

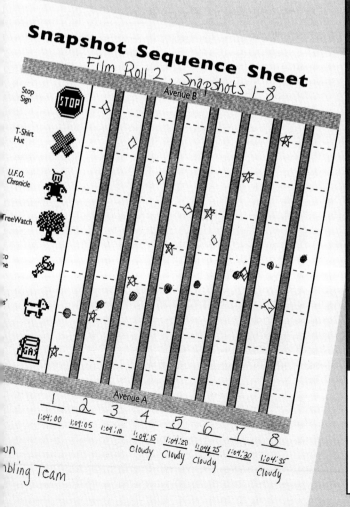

# 4 The Parade Continues

FINDING DATA FROM
A SNAPSHOT
SEQUENCE

**Things have changed at the parade.** There are new characters on the scene, and Monica Chang, the "Eye in the Sky," is having a hard time making her news report. Can you help Monica figure out what's going on?

## Find Missing Data

**How can you determine unknown positions on a snapshot sequence?**

Read Monica's report below, Reporting Live from the Clouds. Then read the handout Latasha's Field Notes II. Notice that clouds prevented Latasha from taking notes some of the time. On a Snapshot Sequence Sheet, fill in the picture number and the time for each photograph. Then record the positions of the tumbling team, the clown, and the pig in each snapshot. What would JT's pictures have looked like if the clouds had not blocked the view in the 4th, 5th, 6th, and 8th pictures?

### Reporting Live from the Clouds

"This is Monica Chang, again, bringing you live coverage of the parade from our Eye on the Scene hot air balloon. We're still looking down on Main Street, between Avenue A and Avenue B. JT has just loaded his camera with a new roll of film, and we're awaiting the next group of parade characters to come into our view."

"Now, JT, it's gotten pretty cloudy all of a sudden," says Monica, "Do you think you'll be able to take any good pictures?"

"I hope so, Monica. The clouds are going to make it difficult for me to take pictures, and for Latasha to see what's going on well enough to take notes, but they seem to be moving in and out, so I should be able to get a clear view for at least some of the pictures."

"Well, JT, get your camera ready. I can just barely see a clown on a skateboard approaching the Gas Station, and just behind her I think I see the Twisted Toes Tumbling Team turning cartwheels. They must be getting dizzy! And...what's that? There's a pig heading from the Stop Sign at Avenue B toward the Gas Station! That's strange. Maybe it escaped from the Creature Corral Petting Farm float."

*Writing Your Own Snapshot Story was a very enlightening activity to me as a teacher. Some students had a difficult time moving to the representational stage. Some very concrete students even saw the snapshot diagram as a picture of a building or a race track with the vertical lines marking the lanes.* ☐

*It was fun listening to different students read their stories. Some were very creative. One student wrote imaginatively about three crocodiles cruising up and down a river hunting for food prospects, such as nature photographers. But quite a few students used the same basic context, where A, B, and C are three people who go to the mall and 1–5 are stores at the mall.* ☐

*student page*

## 3 Imagining Using a Faster Camera

Distribute another Snapshot Sequence Sheet to each student. After the activity, discuss answers. The class should find that the pig ran past the clown in the opposite direction at 2 m/sec, the clown moved forward at 3 m/sec, the tumbling team moved forward at 1 m/sec. The clown and the pig crossed paths when they were 9 m past TreeWatch, at 1:04:18 P.M.

As an extension you may wish to ask the following question: How could you use the positions of the characters at 1:04:20 on your first sequence sheet to check your solution? (Answer: The final positions on the 1-second interval sequence should be the same as the positions at 1:04:20 on the first sequence sheet.)

*student page*

## 4 Writing Your Own Snapshot Story

Distribute a copy of Snapshot Stories, Reproducible R9, to each student. Explain that students should write a creative story or set of field notes and fill in the time and distance parameters consistent with the positions of characters A, B, and C at each snapshot. To do so, they need to decide on a context and characters for the story (e.g., bikes on a path, cars on a road, a street fair). They also need to determine speeds of the characters, times between snapshots, roadside landmarks, and distances between landmarks.

To help students get started, ask the following questions:

- What do the symbols A, B, and C represent? What are A, B, and C doing?

- What do the squares represent?

- What does each picture represent?

## 5 Discussing the Snapshot Sequence Representation

Use the following discussion questions to review the investigation.

- How can you tell which direction the objects are traveling?

- How can you tell when one object is traveling faster than another? (Answer: Symbols of the faster object will lie on a steeper line.)

- How can you figure out the speeds at which objects are traveling? (Answer: Divide the distance traveled by the time it took to do it.)

- How can you tell what probably happened between two snapshots?

- Can you tell what probably happened after the last snapshot?

- Are there things you might want to know about how the characters moved that you cannot tell from the snapshot sequence? (Possible response: Did the characters maintain a constant speed?)

**DO STUDENTS' SNAPSHOT SEQUENCES SHOW:**

- *ability to identify direction, change in speed, and distance traveled by each parade character?*
- *correct placement of parade characters during the intervals where clouds obscured the view of the parade?*

**See *Mathematics of Motion* Assessment pages A6–A7 for assessment information.**

## ADDITIONAL assessment
### O p t i o n s

- **Assessment Rubric,** page A7
- **Phase One Student Assessment Criteria,** page R5
- **Phase One Skill Quiz,** page R2
- **Phase One Skill Quiz Answers,** page A8

## Imagine Using a Faster Camera

Assuming the characters are moving at constant rates, what happened to the pig and the clown between 1:04:15 P.M. and 1:04:20 P.M.? Imagine that you have a faster camera than JT, and you can take a picture every 1 second between 1:04:15 and 1:04:20.

**1** Create a snapshot sequence with a picture every 1 second.

**2** Write an explanation of what happened to the pig and the clown between 1:04:15 P.M. and 1:04:20 P.M.

> **What happens between the snapshots in a snapshot sequence?**

## Write Your Own Snapshot Story

Write a story explaining the snapshot sequence that your teacher gives you. Use your imagination. Your story can be about anything you want!

**1** Before you write your story, do the following:

**a.** Decide what the story is about. Who or what are Characters A, B, and C? What person, place, or thing is at each marker along the road?

**b.** Decide how much time there is between each snapshot and fill in the time of day that each snapshot was taken.

**c.** Decide how much distance there is between each of the 5 landmarks on the road or path.

**2** Your story should also include information about the directions and speeds of the characters, and why they are moving that way.

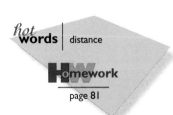

*hot* **words** | distance

**H**W **omework**
page 81

## MATH BACKGROUND

### Distance-Time Graphs

Phase Two focuses on distance-time graphs, a way of representing motion that is widely used in mathematics, physics, and engineering.

The first distance-time graph introduced is the distance-from graph. It shows, at each point in time, how far away the individual is from the starting point. For example, if someone starts at home, walks for an hour at a leisurely pace, rests for a half-hour, and then walks back home at twice the original rate, the distance-from graph would look like the one shown here.

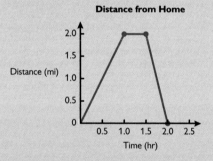

**Distance from Home**

In Lesson 6, students contrast a distance-from graph with a map and a story. For example, the map and story provide information about the specific route taken—where turns were made, and so on—which does not appear on the graph. On the other hand, the map does not show speed, while the slope of the line on a distance-time graph does. This contrast raises a central mathematical question for students to consider: Which representation is best for describing which types of information?

In Lesson 7, students explore two other types of distance-time graphs. One is the total distance graph. It shows the same information as a car odometer. It does not indicate whether something is moving away from or toward the starting point. For the walk described on page 58, the total distance graph would look like this:

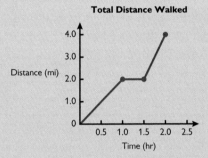

The other graph introduced in this phase is the distance-to graph, which shows, at each point in time, the distance to the destination. This will generally look like the distance-from graph flipped upside down. The distance-to graph for the walk described on page 58 will look like this:

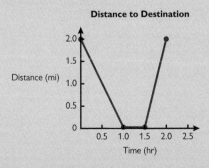

Taken together, these graphs show students that different graphs can show different aspects of the same situation.

Distance-time graphs are powerful: they give you a lot of information in a very compact form. With a distance-time graph, you can quickly see how long it took someone to go someplace, how fast they went, and how far they traveled. You can see, at a glance, which contestant won a race, who lost, and who didn't finish. You can see whether everyone started at the same time, or if somebody had a head start. The distance-time graph is one mathematical tool that belongs in everyone's mathematical tool kit.

# Distance-Time Graphs

## WHAT'S THE MATH?

*Investigations in this section focus on:*

### MEASUREMENT and GEOMETRY

- Setting appropriate scales on graphs
- Interpreting slopes on graphs

### NUMBER and COMPUTATION

- Creating and interpreting distance-time graphs
- Relating different types of distance-time graphs to each other and to stories
- Reading information from maps

### ALGEBRA FUNCTIONS

- Finding distance, time, and speed data in stories

MathScape Online
mathscape3.com/self_check_quiz

# AT A GLANCE

## LESSON 5

# Walk This Way

This lesson introduces students to distance-time graphs. The class collects data on students walking at three different speeds, and creates graphs representing those walks. Students then create graphs using data from prior lessons and information provided in a story.

In this lesson, students work with graphs of distance from a fixed reference point (typically the starting point). In a later lesson, they will be introduced to distance-time graphs that show the total distance traveled over time.

### Mathematical Goals

- Create and interpret distance-time graphs.
- Set appropriate scales on graphs.
- Interpret slopes on graphs.

**MATERIALS**

**PER STUDENT**

- Snapshot sequence records from Lessons 3 and 4
- Reproducible R12
- Reproducible R13 (several copies)

## LESSON 6

# Stories, Maps, and Graphs

This lesson introduces three representations of Jessica's travels through town: (1) a story, (2) a map showing her route, and (3) a distance-time graph. Students use the story, map, and graph to answer a series of questions about Jessica's travels. Then they add a graph showing how Jessica's feelings change over time—an example of a time graph for something other than distance. To complete the lesson, students also create stories, maps, and graphs for their own trips and compare and contrast what types of information are provided by each of these three types of representations.

### Mathematical Goals

- Interpret distance-time graphs.
- Read information from maps.
- Find data in stories.
- Compare different representations.
- Use graphs to show various kinds of changes over time.

**MATERIALS**

**PER STUDENT**

- Reproducible R13 (several copies)
- Reproducible R14

LESSON 7

# A Graphing Matter

This lesson helps students generalize their understanding of how different graphs can be used to show different information about a situation. Students first learn about two new types of distance-time graphs; one type shows the distance to the destination, the other type shows the total distance traveled. They then apply what they have learned to making graphs of walks people take around the room and to converting one type of graph into the others.

## Mathematical Goals

- Create and understand graphs of distance from the starting and ending points.

- Create and understand cumulative distance graphs.

- Use appropriate scales on graphs.

- Relate different types of distance-time graphs to each other and to stories.

**PREPARATION**

In the first step, one student in the class, or one student per group, will need to walk according to the instructions on Student Guide page 64 while the other students in the class or group count the steps and record the time. This can be done in the classroom or in a larger space. Plan where to do this activity.

LESSON 8

# Juan and Marina Go Walking

Students interpret the distance-from, total distance, and hunger/time graphs of Juan and Marina's afternoon walk by writing an imaginative story. They then evaluate each other's work for consistency among the graphs and stories. Finally, they analyze graphs to determine what might be shown and which ones cannot possibly represent a real motion.

## Mathematical Goals

- Interpret graphs of changes over time.

- Combine information from different types of graphs.

- Connect graphs and stories.

- Compare distance-from and total distance graphs.

- Connect graphs to real situations.

# 5

## Introducing Distance-Time Graphs

*After we plotted the points for the end of the walk and the middle of the walk, we talked about ratios and proportions to establish other points on the graph. We also discussed that we were assuming that each student moved at a constant speed throughout the walk.* □

# Walk This Way

Have students review the phase overview on pages 58–59 in the Student Guide.

## 1 Collecting Data to Graph

Measure out a distance for students to walk while others watch and measure the time. The distance should be between 20 and 100 feet—longer is better if space is available. Students can use a piece of tape to mark the starting and ending points.

Ask three students to walk the distance, one at a slow pace, one at a regular pace, and one at a quick pace. Each student should maintain the same pace for the entire distance. Have other students time how long it takes each walker to cover the distance. Be sure to mark 3–4 equally spaced, intermediary points along the way and have students note the time at which each walker passes these points. Keep the data for students to use in making distance-time graphs in Step 3. You may want to keep the data in a data table on the blackboard.

## 2 Learning How to Make Distance-Time Graphs

Give each student a copy of Reproducible 12, Steps in Making a Distance-Time Graph. Then demonstrate the process of creating a distance-time graph. A transparency made from this reproducible can be helpful. You may wish to use the data from the student who walked at the nor-

mal pace. Follow the demonstration with discussion questions.

- What are the important things to remember when deciding what scale to use on the vertical axis of a graph?

- What are the important things to remember when scaling the horizontal axis of a graph?

- How do you plot points on a distance-time graph?

*student page*

## 3 Creating Distance-Time Graphs

Refer students to the investigation and have them make their own distance-time graphs using the data collected from the walks. Each student will need a sheet of graph paper. They may work individually or in groups. As students make their graphs, check that they are choosing appropriate scales and labeling the axes. Also check that they are creating distance-time line graphs, not just plotting individual points.

Each graph should show a straight line, since each student walked at a constant speed. Ask the following questions for closure.

- What features are the same for all three graphs?

- What features vary among the three graphs?

- Why do the graphs all have different slopes?

# homework options

**LESSON HOMEWORK**

*Page 82*

*hot* **topics**

• *Graphing on the Coordinate Plane (6•7)*
  *Exercises 1–11*

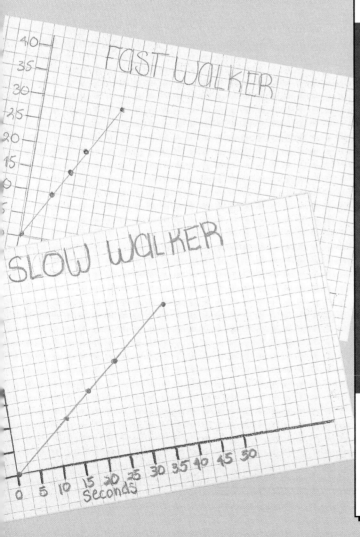

# 5 Walk This Way

INTRODUCING
DISTANCE-TIME
GRAPHS

**As you have discovered, motion can be represented visually in a variety of ways.** There are drawings and maps, and diagrams such as the snapshot sequences you created in Lessons 3 and 4. A graph is another way to represent motion visually.

## Create Distance-Time Graphs

**How can you make graphs representing walks at different speeds?**

Apply what you learned about making distance-time graphs by graphing your data from the three walks at different speeds.

**1** Collect data to graph by working with partners to measure the speeds of a slow walk, a regular walk, and a fast walk.

   **a.** Decide who will walk and who will measure each walk. You must also measure the distance walked and the time it takes in order to calculate the speed.

   **b.** Copy the table, Walks of Various Speeds, to store your data.

**2** Make three distance-time graphs—one for each of the slow, regular, and fast walks. Label the axes to show the distance and time measures.

### Walks of Various Speeds

| | Distance | Time | Speed |
|---|---|---|---|
| Slow | | | |
| Regular | | | |
| Fast | | | |

*We made the first distance-time graph of the three walking speeds, each in a different color, together as a class on the chalkboard. When I asked students if they could tell which person walked the fastest, they had some interesting ideas. I was pleased when Jake suggested, "The blue line is fastest because it went 100 feet in only 10 seconds." I wanted my students to be able to explain why steeper lines are faster, rather than memorize what "steeper" and "flat" lines mean.* ☐

*After he discovered that the steeper the slope of the line, the faster the object is moving, Jamie asked, "How fast would you have to go for the line to go straight up?" This led to an interesting discussion about what a vertical line would mean.* ☐

*When students needed help, I found it useful to refer back to the snapshot sequence diagrams. For example, "How did the snapshot sequences look when someone was not moving at all?" Gradually, students began to see the many parallels between the snapshot sequences and distance-time graphs.* ☐

### 4 Connecting Stories and Graphs

Each student will need graph paper and the Snapshot Sequence Sheets from Lessons 3 and 4. Depending upon which characters students choose, the lines of their parade graphs may change slopes (showing changes in speed), be horizontal for some period (showing that the character had stopped), or have a negative slope (to show the character moving in the opposite direction from that of the parade). Making graphs of this information helps students connect the snapshot sequences with graphs.

The story of Pedro and Tanya introduces a new situation. The second character (Pedro) starts at a different position and at a later time than the first character (Tanya). As shown below, the graph also must indicate that Tanya and Pedro arrived at school at the same time. Students might assume that Pedro and Tanya walk in straight lines on their way to school.

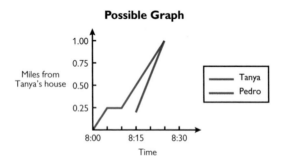

**Possible Graph**

### 5 Relating Graphs to Motion

You may want to discuss the questions from the Student Guide, or they can be answered in writing. Students will continue to explore their graphs in the following lessons, and will have opportunities to deepen their understanding and revisit these questions.

For further follow-up, and to focus on scale and slope, use the following discussion questions.

- How does your graph of the parade characters relate to the snapshot sequences?

- How does a graph show that someone has changed speed?

- How does a graph show when two people are moving in the same direction? in opposite directions?

- How can a graph show that two people started in different places? at different times?

- How does a distance-time graph show that someone has not moved for some time?

# what to look for

**DO STUDENTS' GRAPHS SHOW:**

• *correctly scaled and labeled axes?*

• *correctly plotted points?*

• *full utilization of space available to make graphs easy to read?*

• *slopes drawn correctly through points rather than line segments connecting points in a dot-to-dot fashion?*

**See** *Mathematics of Motion* **Assessment page A9 for assessment information.**

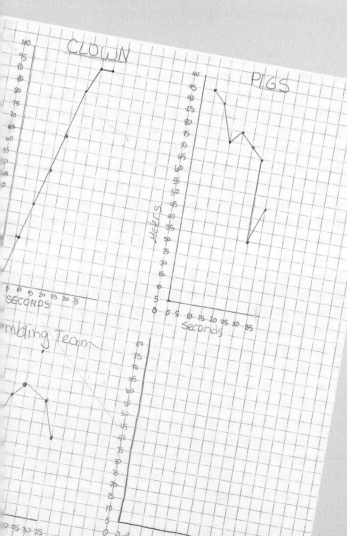

## Connect Stories and Graphs

Sometimes, data is gathered from an experiment before it is graphed. Other times, graphs can be prepared from information given in a story.

**1** Choose any three of the characters in the parade in Lessons 3 and 4 and make a distance-time graph showing how they moved. Remember to label the axes to show the distance and time measures.

**2** Read the story "Tanya and Pedro's Trips to School." Create a graph to show what happens in the story. Be sure your graph shows about how far each person went and how much time they spent.

> **How can you make a distance-time graph to represent the activities of characters in a story?**

### Tanya and Pedro's Trips to School

Tanya's house is 1 mile away from her school. She started out to school at 8:00 A.M. On her way to school, Tanya walked for 5 minutes, going about $\frac{1}{4}$ of a mile. She then spent 5 minutes waiting for her friend Pedro. Pedro wasn't ready, and Tanya was worried that she would be late

for school. She walked for 15 more minutes to get to school.

Pedro started from his house and ran to school in 10 minutes. He got there at the same time as Tanya arrived.

## Relate Graphs to Motion

Write your answers to these questions about the distance-time graphs you made.

▪ How did you decide what scale to use on the axis of each of your graphs?

▪ If you used a different scale, how would your graph change? How would it stay the same?

▪ Are all the lines on your graphs straight? Why or why not?

▪ When two lines are on the same graph, what does it tell you when one is steeper than the other? Why?

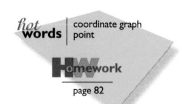

*hot* **words** | coordinate graph, point

**H****omework** page 82

## Comparing and Contrasting Representations

*I reviewed the basics of reading maps and graphs with my class before they started the activity. Some of my students weren't familiar with maps showing city blocks, so it was good that we reviewed this in advance. ☐*

*We had a lively discussion about whether it is preferable to use a map or written directions when you need to find an unfamiliar place. The class was just about split down the middle. We decided that a good map and good directions are both fine ways to get someplace new, and it's strictly a matter of personal preference. ☐*

# Stories, Maps, and Graphs

*student page*

## 1 Interpreting a Story, Map, and Graph

Call students' attention to the map, graph, and story describing Jessica's travels. Encourage students to mentally trace along the map and graph as they follow Jessica's progress through the story. They should recognize that the graph shows Jessica's distance from home, given as numbers of blocks, during her hour of traveling. Pose the following discussion questions and accept general answers.

- How do stories, maps, and graphs differ?

- What kind of information does each representation show best?

- What does the horizontal axis of the graph represent? What does its vertical axis represent? (Answers: Time of day, Blocks from home)

Give each student a copy of Stories, Maps, and Graphs: What Was Jessica Doing, Reproducible R14, and have students complete the writing exercise to answer the question, "What was Jessica doing?" Next, you may wish to pose the preceding discussion questions again to see how students revise their answers in light of what they have learned.

This activity provides an opportunity to discuss the idea that the representation you prefer depends upon what information you need. It also helps students realize how a graph is different from a picture or map of a motion.

**LESSON HOMEWORK**

*Page 83*

Repro. 11

*[handwritten notes]*

It is 4 blocks. My answer is approximate and I used the map. I counted the blocks to find my answer

a. Jessica spent a approximate tim... used the graph and estim...

b. Jessica bought... used the gr... min. I

c. ...

...essica stayed in one place when she was at the grocery store, when she looked for her friends, and when she waited for her brother to drink his milk. This answer is approximate and I read and looked at the graph.

Jessica was traveling further away from home when she headed towards the school. This is exact and I looked on the map.

L. Jessica was getting closer to home when she was commin back from the store. This is exact and I used the map.

m. Jessica was traveling fastest going to the store. She was traveling slowest comming home from the store. This answer is approximate and I estimated on the graph.

n. the park and grocery store are both the same distance to Jessica's house. This answer is exact and I used the map

---

## 6 Stories, Maps, and Graphs

COMPARING AND CONTRASTING REPRESENTATIONS

**As you know, there are several useful ways to represent information about motion.** Stories, maps, and graphs are some of these ways. But do stories, maps, and graphs provide the same information? Are they all equally useful?

### Interpret a Story, Map, and Graph

Read the story, map, and graph about Jessica's travels. Then answer the questions on the sheet your teacher will give you that asks what Jessica was doing.

**Information About Jessica's Travels**

Jessica lives at the corner of 1st Street and Avenue A. She was planning to meet her friends at 10:30 A.M. at the school.

At 10:00 A.M., her mother asked her to go to the corner grocery store to get milk for her brother. She jumped on her bike and rushed out, biking two blocks along Avenue A and then going on 3rd Street to the grocery store.

She grabbed the milk and went to the express line. There were several people in front of her, so she had to wait.

When she left the grocery store, she discovered she had a flat tire. She walked her bike home along Avenue C and 1st Street. When she got home, she had to wait for her brother to drink his milk. Then her mother drove her to school, but she was late, and her friends weren't there. Her mother drove her to the park to look for her friends. She finally caught up to her friends at the park at 11:00 A.M.

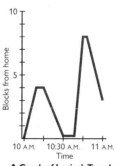

**A Map of Jessica's Travels**

**A Graph of Jessica's Travels**

*Students were very creative here. Stories ranged from an adaptation of Little Red Riding Hood to a story of a dog's travels during a day, to journeys into outer space (including, of course, lots of trips to the mall also). I gave extra help to several students who were still working out their understandings of distance-time graphs because I found that their graphs were not always completely consistent with their stories and maps.* □

*Sharing and checking were valuable. Students were able to see how others drew their maps and graphs, and why it was important to do them carefully. They quickly noted, for example, that they could not check for consistency between the graph and story if the axes of the graph were not properly labeled.* □

*student page*

## 2 Graphing Other Things That Change Over Time

Graphs can be used to show many other things that change over time besides distance. Students are now asked to make a graph showing how Jessica felt during the course of the story. Instead of distance along the *y*-axis, students might put happiness, annoyance, or any other feeling they think Jessica might have had during the events in the story.

Any graph that shows some correspondence to the story—for example, shows different feelings at the time Jessica discovered she had a flat tire and the time she found her friends—is an appropriate answer to this question. The key point here is for students to begin generalizing the use of time graphs to include things other than distance.

Afterwards the class could discuss the following questions.

- In what way was a graph well suited to representing Jessica's feelings?
- In what way was a graph not well suited to representing Jessica's feelings?
- Is there a better way to represent Jessica's feelings? If so, how?

*student page*

## 3 Creating Stories, Maps, and Graphs

Each student selects a trip he or she knows well or a fantasy trip. Students write a description, draw a map, make a distance-time graph, and make a graph showing their feelings during the trip. When students finish their stories, maps, and graphs, have them exchange their work with a partner's and check each other for consistency. They can write answers to each of the following questions about their partner's work.

- Do the times in the story match those in the graph?
- Do the distances shown on the map match those on the graph?
- Does the graph of feelings match the events in the story?
- Are the story and map consistent?

Have students share their critiques of one another's work.

## 4 Discussing the Uses of Graphs, Maps, and Stories

Discuss which representations show distance, time, routes, speeds, and other information about a trip.

- What kinds of information are easiest to get from a graph? from a map? from a story?
- What kinds of information can you find in all three representations?

# what to look for

**DOES STUDENTS' WORK SHOW:**

- *ability to count blocks to determine distance on the city block map?*
- *understanding that various changes over time can be graphed as functions of time?*
- *facility with all three kinds of representations: stories, maps, and graphs?*

**See *Mathematics of Motion* Assessment page A9 for assessment information.**

## Centimeter Grid Paper

How Jessica Felt (Her Happiness)

## Graph Other Things That Change Over Time

Graphs can be used to show how an object's position—or almost anything else—changes over time. Draw a graph that shows how Jessica felt during different times in the story. You can graph how happy she felt, how annoyed, or any feeling you choose.

**What kinds of changes over time can be shown on a graph?**

## Create Stories, Maps, and Graphs

Choose a trip that you are familiar with, or make up a fantasy trip. For your trip, do each of the following.

- Write a description or story.
- Draw a map.
- Make a distance-time graph.
- Make one other graph showing how you or a character in your story felt during the trip.

**What kinds of travels can you describe with a story, map, and graph?**

*hot* **words** | graph
picture graph

**H**W**omework**

page 83

**MATHEMATICS OF MOTION** • LESSON 6    **63**

10:20   10:30   10:40   10:50

# 7

## Making Three Types of Distance-Time Graphs

*Several of my students observed that Graph B is like Graph A, but inverted, and were curious why. We discussed that the reason is that as the mover gets farther from the starting point, he or she gets closer to the ending point. So one of these graphs can be made from the other just by "flipping" the lines over. □*

# A Graphing Matter

*student page*

## 1 Making Three Types of Distance-Time Graphs

In this investigation, one student walks while others make graphs showing the number of steps the mover is from the starting point, the number of steps from the ending point, and the total number of steps taken. That is, students create graphs showing the distance from the starting point, distance to the end point, and total distance traveled, with each distance measured by the number of steps.

Students should be divided into groups of four. Alternatively, you could play the role of the mover and arrange students in groups of three, with each student choosing to make Graph A, B, or C.

## 2 Comparing Graphs A, B, and C

For follow-up to the investigation, have students respond to the following questions. They can be used for discussion or as a written exercise.

- How are Graph A and Graph B alike? How are they different? (Answers: They slope up and down at the same angles; every upward slope in Graph A is matched by a downward slope in Graph B.)

- How can you tell whether a distance-from graph (Graph A) and a distance-to graph (Graph B) show the same motion? (Answer: They are mirror images.)

- How are Graph A and Graph C alike? How are they different? (Answers: They both consist of straight line segments; Graph C never slopes downward, while Graph A goes up and down.)

- How can you tell whether a distance-from graph (Graph A) and a total distance graph (Graph C) show the same motion? (Answer: They are the same if the upward slopes are the same at corresponding points, and if the downward slopes in Graph A are inverted in Graph C at corresponding points.)

- Why does Graph C never slope downward? (Answer: When direction of movement is ignored, total distance moved cannot be reduced over time.)

**Centimeter Grid Paper**

GRAPH A - DISTANCE FROM

6 8 10 12 14 16 18 20 22 24 26 28 30 32
Time (seconds)

# 7 A Graphing Matter

**MAKING THREE TYPES OF DISTANCE-TIME GRAPHS**

**Distance-time graphs come in several different sorts.**
You've had some experience with graphs that show how far something is from its starting point. Now you will learn how to make two other useful distance-time graphs.

## Make Three Types of Distance-Time Graphs

**What are some useful kinds of distance-time graphs?**

In this activity, you and your partners will make three different kinds of graphs—Graph A, Graph B, and Graph C. Either your teacher or someone in your group will be the mover.

**1** The mover does the following: Select a place where you can walk in a straight line while the others watch. When walking, walk at a steady pace. Others will need to count the number of steps you take, so don't go too quickly. When everyone is ready:

a. Walk from the starting point to the ending point.

b. Wait for about 5 seconds.

c. Walk halfway back to the starting point.

d. Wait about 5 seconds.

e. Walk back to the ending point.

f. Wait about 5 seconds.

g. Walk back to the starting point.

**2** Make the graphs. Each member of the group should make a different graph—either A, B, or C. Each graph will show something different about the number of steps the mover has taken. Graph A shows how many steps the mover is from the starting point throughout the walking time. Graph B shows how many steps the mover is from the ending point throughout the walking time. Graph C shows the total number of steps the mover has taken throughout the walking time.

*I was glad I let my students develop their own paths to measure—there were lots of clever choices. One group chose a circular path to see what its graph would look like. They discovered that if you move in a circle with the reference point in the center, the distance-from graph is flat—like the graphs they had seen before of constant position. □*

*To keep things clear, I told my students in advance that all travel occurred along the streets shown in the map: Jessica didn't take any shortcuts going diagonally across any of the blocks. We also agreed that all of the blocks were square. □*

*student page*

## 3 Graphing New Routes

For additional practice in creating the three types of distance-time graphs, plan some walking paths in the classroom, or ask students to plan some paths. Divide the class into three groups, with each group making one type of graph for each walk. As you or a student walks a path, the rest of the class collects the information they need to make their graphs. The walker may need to walk the path several times to enable everyone to collect the information.

Rotate which type of graph each group is to make, so that everyone gets practice with all three types.

For follow-up, you can ask the following discussion questions.

- On your graph, how did you determine the distance from the ending point?

- How did you determine total distance?

 For students to be able to graph distance from the end point, they will need to calibrate the path before walking. Alternatively, students could simply estimate the distance from the ending point.

*student page*

## 4 Converting Among Types of Graphs

Ask students to refer to Student Guide page 62 in Lesson 6, which contains the story, map, and graph of Jessica's travels. Explain that they will make three graphs, as described on the student page. Creating these graphs will further reinforce the idea that different graphs can show different information about the same situation. Possible discussion questions are given below.

- How did you determine the total distance Jessica traveled?

- How did you figure out how Jessica's distance changed over time?

- How did you determine how Jessica's distance from the park changed over time?

# what to look for

**DO STUDENTS' GRAPHS:**

- *use appropriate scales?*
- *show nondecreasing slope (for cumulative distance graphs)?*
- *appear to be mirror images (Graphs A and B)?*
- *reflect important details of the stories they represent?*

**See *Mathematics of Motion* Assessment page A9 for assessment information.**

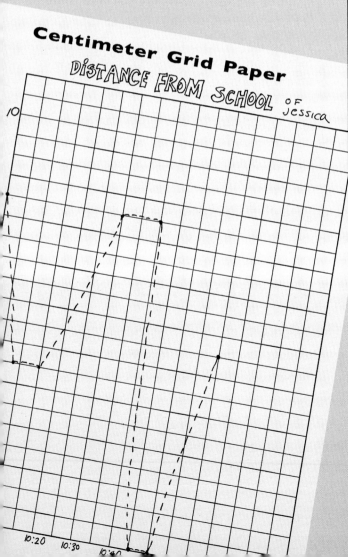

Centimeter Grid Paper

DISTANCE FROM SCHOOL of Jessica

## Graph New Routes

Practice making the three kinds of distance-time graphs with new walking paths.

**1** Decide who will be the mover and what the mover's path will be. If your teacher doesn't provide a path, make one up. Here is an example:

**a.** Start at the door to the classroom.

**b.** Walk slowly to the teacher's desk.

**c.** Wait 10 seconds.

**d.** Walk quickly to the bookcase.

**2** Decide which graph you will make. Make either an A graph (distance from the starting point), a B graph (distance to the end point), or a C graph (total distance).

**3** Watch the walker walk the path and gather the data you need to make your graph. Make your A, B, or C graph.

**4** Repeat the process twice more but rotate which graph you make, so that each member of your group makes each kind of graph.

## Convert Among Types of Graphs

Using the story, map, and graph of Jessica's travels from Lesson 6, page 62, create each of the following graphs:

- a graph showing the total distance Jessica traveled
- a graph showing how Jessica's distance from the school changed over time
- a graph showing how Jessica's distance from the park changed over time

> Can you make three kinds of distance-time graphs for new walking routes?

*hot* **words** | total distance graph distance-from graph

**Homework** page 84

## Interpreting Graphs of Motion

*At first, there were quite a few students who didn't read the scales carefully enough to realize that Juan and Marina walked at the same speed! We discussed how you could make stories in which they walked together the whole way, walked together for part of the way, or did not walk together at all. In our final discussions we agreed that as Juan and Marina always walked at the same speed, it was highly likely that they stayed together. □*

*One student explored what would happen if you flew east to west, crossing time zones so fast that you arrived in California at an earlier time than you left New York. That led to a discussion of the difference between elapsed time and the actual clock time where you are. □*

# Juan and Marina Go Walking

*student page*

## 1 Writing a Story to Match Four Graphs

The set of graphs can be interpreted in many different ways. Students should notice, however, that Juan's graph shows distance from a reference point, while Marina's shows total distance, and the scales of the graphs differ. The following interpretations are possible.

- Marina walks 12 miles and ends up 12 miles from home. Juan takes a completely separate walk.

- Juan and Marina walk together for the first half of their walk and then go their separate ways. Marina continues on a circular walk and ends up at home, while Juan retraces his steps home.

- Juan and Marina stay together on a circular route.

- Juan and Marina stay together and both retrace their steps.

If students are having difficulty, you may want to ask the following discussion questions before they do the investigation. Or you can write the questions on the blackboard, unanswered, to guide students' thinking.

- Is Juan's graph a total distance graph or a distance-from graph? Which is Marina's?

(Answers: distance-from; It could be either distance-from or total distance.)

- Why does Juan's graph first slope upward then downward? (Answer: He goes first away from home, then toward home.)

- Why do both Marina's and Juan's graphs have flat portions? (Answer: They are not moving for a while.)

- Are the scales of Marina's and Juan's graphs the same? (Answer: No)

## 2 Sharing and Checking

Arrange students in pairs and have partners exchange stories. Tell each student to do the following to their partner's story:

- Underline all statements that are directly connected to the graphs. (For example, that Juan set out at 2 P.M.)

- Circle any statements or parts of the map that are not consistent with the graph or story. That is, circle anything that you think is an error.

# 8 Juan and Marina Go Walking

INTERPRETING
GRAPHS OF MOTION

**"A picture is worth a thousand words."** Have you ever heard that saying? As you will see in this lesson, graphs are pictures that can contain a lot of information in a compact form.

What story can you write based on four different graphs?

## Write a Story to Match Four Graphs

Write an imaginative story that matches the information on the graphs below. Use information from all four of the graphs.

### Juan's and Marina's Walks

**Juan's Graphs**

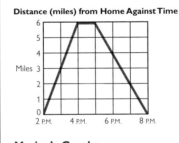

Distance (miles) from Home Against Time

How Hungry Against Time

**Marina's Graphs**

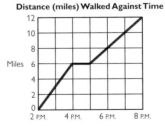

Distance (miles) Walked Against Time

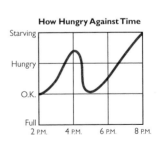

How Hungry Against Time

*For graph (g), Chantal wrote about a boy who was being chased by an alligator, and ran in a "zig-zag" to get away. Jesse suggested an improvement to her story that included more information about the point of reference and the directions the characters are moving, "You're running away from an alligator, but turn back toward where you started. The alligator snaps at you so start running away again." □*

*I was surprised to find that some students still confused graphs and pictures. For example, one student saw the graphs as roads up a mountain. She drew pictures of a car on each graph. She concluded that graphs (d), (h), and (i) were impossible because "the car would fall off the road." The amazing thing is that this strategy gave her the correct answers. If I hadn't seen her drawings and found out what she was thinking, I would have thought she understood! □*

### 3 Finding the Impossible Graphs

Students are given a set of distance-time graphs without scales on the axes. They are first asked to decide which graphs could show total distance traveled. Students should find that graphs (a), (c), (e), (f), and perhaps (i), show total distance traveled, since distance never decreases on those graphs. Students are then asked which graphs are impossible. Here, students should find that graphs (d), (h), and perhaps (i), are impossible, since they show the object at two or more places at the same time, or they show time moving backwards.

You may want students to draw their own impossible graphs as a follow-up to the investigation.

> If graph (i) is seen as going straight up, it is impossible, since it would show that the object moved while time did not. However, graph (i) could also be seen as showing an extremely rapid movement, so that distance is covered in such a small amount of time that you cannot see the time change on the graph. If students raise these different views, ask them to draw what they think an enlarged version of this graph would look like. You should be able to see the differences on an enlarged version of the graph.

### 4 Writing Science Fiction from Impossible Graphs

As an extra challenge, give the students the following assignment:

- Make up a science fiction story that makes one of the impossible graphs possible.

After students have written their stories, ask volunteers to share them. For each story, the class can discuss the following question: Is the science fiction story consistent with the graph?

If you wish, you can compile the stories as a binder of "collected works." The binder can be checked out like a library book, so that students can review one another's work. You might want to give extra credit to students who check out the binder, read the stories, and write a response to the following question: Which story is the best science fiction interpretation of a graph? Why?

# assessment criteria

## DID THE STUDENT:

- *recognize that total distance graphs cannot show a decrease in distance at any point, but distance-from graphs can?*
- *recognize that some graphs are impossible because they would require the mover to be in two places at the same time or move backwards in time?*
- *give stories for the other graphs that are consistent with the direction and relative speed of the motion shown on the graph?*

**See *Mathematics of Motion* Assessment pages A10–A11 for assessment information.**

## ADDITIONAL assessment Options

- **Assessment Rubric,** page A11
- **Phase Two Student Assessment Criteria,** page R5
- **Phase Two Skill Quiz,** page R3
- **Phase Two Skill Quiz Answers,** page A12

## Find the Impossible Graphs

Examine the distance-time graphs shown. Then answer the following questions.

**1** Which of the graphs below could show total distance traveled? How did you decide?

**2** Some of the other graphs could show distance from a starting point, but some of them cannot possibly be correct! Which graphs cannot represent the journey of a single person or vehicle? Why?

**3** For each of the graphs that is possible, describe in one sentence what the graph might show. For example, could any of the graphs represent throwing a ball? riding a bike?

> **Which of the graphs shown are impossible?**

## Write Science Fiction from Impossible Graphs

Extra challenge: Make up a science fiction story that makes one of the impossible graphs possible.

**Distance-Time Graphs**

| a | b | c |
| d | e | f |
| g | h | i |

(axes labeled Distance vs. Time)

hotwords | dependent events

Homework
page 85

# PHASE THREE

To: Channel KMTH Sports Announcers

The station has purchased a new graph-making computer to help you with your sports announcements. The computer creates graphs that show distance versus time and speed versus time for running races, swimming races, and other sports events. The graphs allow you to give more precise information to your television viewers. Practice reading the graphs of the races, for they will provide much interesting information—if your graph-reading skills are up to it!

### Average Speed

In this final phase, students extend their knowledge to include speed-time graphs and the concept of average speed.

Average speed is considered both graphically and numerically. For example, the following graph shows a runner in a race. In Lesson 9, we consider the idea of a robot that can be programmed at one speed for the entire race. At what speed should we program the robot so that it ends up in a tie with the runner?

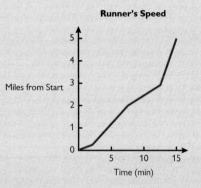

**Runner's Speed**

One approach is to find the total distance run and the time and calculate the average speed according to the formula, $s = d \div t$. If we then show the robot's race on the graph, it will be a straight line, since the speed was constant, and the line should start and end at the same distance and time points as the runner, since we want the race to be a tie.

**Runner's and Robot's Speeds**

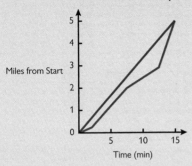

## Comparing Distance-Time and Speed-Time Graphs

Speed-time graphs are very different from distance-time graphs. When speed is constant, the distance-time graph goes up at a constant rate. But on a speed-time graph, this would be shown as a flat line. If the line goes up, it means acceleration is taking place; if it goes down, braking is taking place. However, the scale of the graph may be too large for a brief interval of acceleration or braking to be seen.

## Applying Prior Lessons

In this phase, students also apply all they have learned in a variety of activities, including creating graphs of real motions (Lesson 10), using calculations and formulas to compare average speeds of Olympic record-setting runners (Lesson 11), translating among the different types of graphs (Lesson 11), and analyzing a motion that they select (Lesson 12).

Who will make it first to the finish line? Graphs and equations allow you to see patterns that help you predict the results of a race. Using mathematics allows you to do much more than predict the outcome of a race. With the techniques you will learn in this phase, you can calculate how long it will take to ride your bike someplace you have never been before, or how fast you should walk to get to your friend's house in 10 minutes.

# Using Graphs to Solve Problems

## WHAT'S THE MATH?

*Investigations in this section focus on:*

### MEASUREMENT and GEOMETRY

- Determining or estimating average speeds

### NUMBER and COMPUTATION

- Interpreting and creating distance-time graphs
- Interpreting and creating speed-time graphs
- Relating distance-time and speed-time graphs
- Comparing constant and variable speeds on distance-time graphs

### ALGEBRA FUNCTIONS

- Applying graphs to solving problems
- Applying equations relating distance, time, and speed to solving problems
- Applying average speed to solving problems

MathScape Online
**mathscape3.com/self_check_quiz**

# AT A GLANCE

LESSON 9

# The Race Announcer

Students are given a graph of a race. From the graph, they create a commentary describing the race. Students then exchange commentaries and see if a partner can recreate the original graph from the commentary. Students then explore how to determine the average speed of a runner.

## Mathematical Goals

- Interpret and create distance-time graphs.
- Determine average speeds.
- Compare constant and variable speeds on distance-time graphs.

**MATERIALS**

**PER STUDENT**

- Reproducible R13 (several copies)
- Reproducible R15

LESSON 10

# How Fast? How Far? How Long?

Students are given a story of a family on a trip and four graphs. They figure out what each graph shows and label and scale the vertical axes accordingly. Then they choose three different motions and make a distance-time graph and a speed-time graph of each. They explore the question, "How does a speed-time graph compare with a distance-time graph of the same motion?"

**MATERIALS**

**PER STUDENT**

- Reproducible R13 (several copies)

## Mathematical Goals

- Interpret and create speed-time graphs.
- Relate distance-time and speed-time graphs.
- Determine or estimate average speeds.

# LESSON 11

# The Race Is On!

Students perform calculations to determine average speed and other motion parameters for women's marathon races. They also use the distance equation to solve various algebra problems involving motion. Finally, they are given a graph showing the pattern of motion of three unspecified movers and are asked to write an accompanying story and create total distance and speed-time graphs.

## Mathematical Goals

- Apply graphs to solve problems.
- Apply equations relating distance, time, and speed to solving problems.
- Apply average speed to solve problems.

### MATERIALS

#### PER STUDENT

- Reproducible R13 (several copies)
- Reproducible R16

# LESSON 12

# Final Project

Students collect and analyze data, solve problems, and make graphs related to some motion of their own choosing. They apply all of the graphing skills they have learned in the unit and use the distance equation to produce some finished work, of unspecified format, that reflects what they have learned.

## Mathematical Goals

- Apply the distance equation to calculate average speed and solve problems.
- Create distance-from, distance-to, total distance, and speed-time graphs.
- Use various methods, including stories, graphs, and maps, to represent the same motion.
- Distinguish between and apply average speed and peak speed.

### MATERIALS

#### PER STUDENT

- various supplies from the following list, depending on the nature of students' investigations: graph paper; colored markers; pencils or paints; poster board; magazines; encyclopedias; almanacs; computer with Internet access or graphing software; physics apparatus, such as an air track; balls; ramps; stopwatches; metersticks and other measuring instruments

**Converting Words to Graphs and Back Again**

*My students really captured the flavor of a play-by-play sports commentary. Their reports began with phrases like, "And they're off...."*

*At first, some of my students thought that the point where the two lines cross in the swimming race represented the two swimmers crashing. But Erica quickly pointed out that swimmers swim in separate lanes, so the crossing lines represented the swimmers passing each other.*

*When my students paired up and tried to draw graphs from each other's commentaries, some realized that their reports didn't have enough details. I had them rewrite their stories to include enough details so that their partners would be able to draw the graphs.* □

# The Race Announcer

Have students review the phase overview on pages 68–69 in the Student Guide.

**student page**

## 1 Playing the Role of a Sports Announcer

Make copies of Reproducible R15, Race Graphs, which features graphs of a swimming race, running race, and three-legged race. Cut the copies into thirds, and distribute one of the three races to each student.

Explain that students will use the graph to create a commentary describing the race. Emphasize that the commentaries must be very detailed and thorough because they will be used to make graphs in the next step. Students can write their commentaries, tape record them, or prepare notes from which they will present them to others.

You may want to post the following questions for students to use as guidelines while they write.

- What are the relative positions of the racers at various times during the race?

- At what times do changes of speed occur?

- Is the speed of each racer constant, or does it vary?

- Who covers the distance in the least time?

When students finish writing their commentaries, have them prepare their graphs based on the commentaries.

Pair students so that partners have worked with different graphs. Have them share their commentaries but not the corresponding graphs. Distribute graph paper so each student can make a graph based upon the other's commentary.

When graphing is complete, have students write responses to the questions. You may want to give partners shared credit for turning in corrected commentaries and graphs.

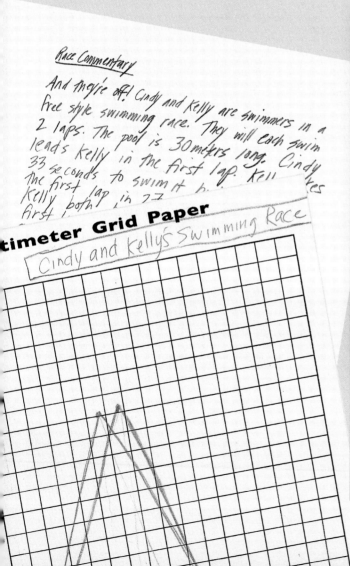

Race Commentary

And they're off! Cindy and Kelly are swimmers in a free style swimming race. They will each swim 2 laps. The pool is 30 meters long. Cindy leads Kelly in the first lap. Cindy takes 33 seconds to swim it ... The first lap in ... Kelly ... Kelly both lap in 77 first ...

timeter Grid Paper

Cindy and Kelly's Swimming Race

# 9 The Race Announcer

CONVERTING
WORDS TO GRAPHS
AND BACK AGAIN

**In a race, do all the runners move at a constant speed?** As sports announcers know, racers normally speed up and slow down as a race progresses. Distance-time graphs also show the changing speeds in a race.

## Play the Role of a Sports Announcer

**How does speed vary during a race?**

You will receive a graph of a running, swimming, or three-legged race. Your job is to write a commentary describing the race. Then your partner will use your commentary to recreate the original distance-time graph of the race.

**1** Imagine that you are the TV announcer for the race. Describe what is happening as fully and as accurately as you can. Be sure your commentary matches the graph. Include enough detail in your commentary so that your partner will be able to make a graph from it.

**2** Work with a partner who wrote a commentary on a different race. Use your partner's commentary to make a distance-time graph. Try to make your graph just like the original one. When you are finished, write your answers to the following questions.

   **a.** How closely does your graph match the original graph? Summarize the features that your graph shares with the original graph. Then, summarize the features that are different in your graph and the original graph.

   **b.** Compare the original graph of the race to the commentary you used to make your graph. Describe any errors the commentary contains. How could they be corrected?

*This problem was more difficult for the swimming race than for the other two, since the racers did not go in one direction. Some students showed two different average speeds, one for before the turn and one for after the turn. Students who used one average speed did it by calculating the total distance (60 meters) by the time of the winner, 58 seconds (approximately).* □

*student page*

## 2 Finding Out How Fast a Robot Should Run

Students are asked to figure out at what speed to program a robot to run so that it will exactly tie a racer. The robot is programmed at a constant speed for the entire race, so it needs to be programmed at the racer's average speed.

Some students may solve this problem using the equation: average speed = total distance ÷ total time. Others may plot the robot's race on a graph and then figure out the speed from the graph.

Before students begin the investigation, the following discussion questions can be used as a warm-up.

- If Antonio's speed were constant, what would the graph look like? (Answer: A straight line)

- Is the robot's speed equal to Antonio's during any part of the race? (Answer: No)

- What is Antonio's average speed during the race? (Answer: 0.333 miles/min)

 Answers to investigation question 5 are: to tie runner, 8.0 m/sec; to tie swimmer, 1.03 m/sec; to tie three-legged team, 0.39 m/sec.

## 3 Discussing Average Speed

The following discussion questions can be used to further develop the concept of average speed.

- Is the robot's speed equal to Antonio's at any time besides the starting and ending times of the race? (Answer: No)

- Do the robot and Antonio have the same average speed? (Answer: Yes)

- Is the average speed of an object necessarily equal to its speed at particular points in its motion? Can it be equal? (Answers: No; Yes)

- How can average speed be defined? (Possible answers: total speed divided by total time; middle speed between fastest and slowest, and so on.)

- How can average speed be determined with an equation? with a distance-time graph? (Answers: average speed $= \frac{\text{total distance}}{\text{total time}}$; average speed is the slope of a line drawn between the initial and final points of the graph.)

- How can you calculate average speed for an object that changes direction (such as the swimmers in the race)? (Answer: Divide total distance by time.)

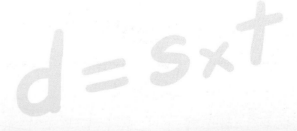

# what to look for

**DO STUDENTS:**

- *include enough detail in their commentaries so that graphs can be created from them?*
- *have a definite method for determining average speed?*
- *correctly determine total distance for the swimming race by adding the forward and return laps of the swimmers?*
- *recognize that Team A did not complete the three-legged race?*

**See *Mathematics of Motion* Assessment page A13 for assessment information.**

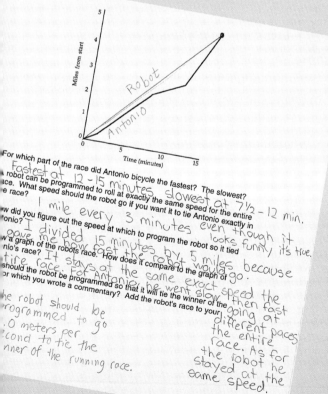

*For which part of the race did Antonio bicycle the fastest? The slowest?*

Fastest at 12-15 minutes, slowest at 7½-12 min.

*A robot can be programmed to roll at exactly the same speed for the entire race. What speed should the robot go if you want it to tie Antonio exactly in the race?*

1 mile every 3 minutes even though it looks funny, it's true.

*How did you figure out the speed at which to program the robot so it tied Antonio?* I gave me the how fast the robot would go. I divided 15 minutes by 5 miles because

*Draw a graph of the robot's race. How does it compare to the graph of Antonio's race?* It stays at the same exact speed the entire race. For Antonio he went slow then fast going at different paces the entire race. As for the robot he stayed at the same speed.

*How should the robot be programmed so that it will tie the winner of the race for which you wrote a commentary? Add the robot's race to your*

The robot should be programmed to go .0 meters per :cond to tie the nner of the running race.

---

## Find Out How Fast a Robot Should Run

The following graph shows how Antonio bicycled in a five-mile race. Use the graph to answer the questions below.

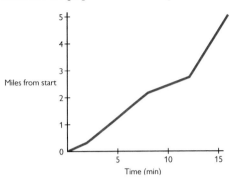

**1** For which part of the race did Antonio bicycle the fastest? the slowest?

**2** A robot can be programmed to roll at exactly the same speed for the entire race. How fast should the robot go if you want it to tie Antonio exactly in the race?

**3** How did you figure out the speed at which to program the robot so it tied Antonio?

**4** Draw a graph of the robot's race. How does it compare to the graph of Antonio's race?

**5** How should the robot be programmed so that it will tie the winner of the race for which you wrote a commentary? Add the robot's race to your graph.

> At what speed should you program a robot so it ties Antonio in a race?

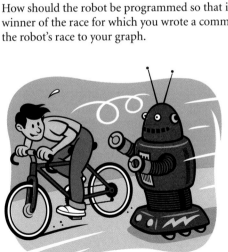

**hot words**
average
average speed
total distance graph

**Homework**
page 86

# 10

**LESSON**

## Exploring Speed-Time Graphs

*We had a discussion about how "real" the speed-time graph could be, since it would take time to speed up and slow down, and it is unlikely that they would drive at exactly the same speed for an hour. By raising these questions, students demonstrated that they understood the graph. We agreed that the time it takes to speed up or slow down would be too small to see on a graph this size. We also agreed that the graph showed the average speed during each interval, not how the speed changed minute by minute.* □

# How Fast? How Far? How Long?

*student page*

## 1 Problem Solving with New Kinds of Graphs

Students are given a story of a family on a trip and four graphs. They figure out what each graph shows and label and scale the vertical axes accordingly.

Two of the graphs should be very familiar. Graph A shows distance from home; Graph C shows total distance traveled. Graph B could show the hunger level of the members of the family—it peaks just before lunch and drops quickly as the family has lunch. Or students may have other, equally plausible ideas about what this graph shows. Graph D shows the speed at which the family travels over each period of time. This is a new type of graph. It shows the miles-per-hour at which the family is traveling during each time interval.

For students who are having difficulty, you may wish to ask the following discussion questions.

- What does it mean if a graph that shows change over time is flat? (Answer: The graph is constant.)

- What does it mean if the graph never slopes downward? (Answer: The graph does not decrease over time.)

- What can a graph that has the same values at the starting and ending points represent? (Answer: If it is a distance graph, it could show a round trip.)

The speed-time graph helps students recognize an important feature of all graphs that show change over time: If whatever is measured is not changing, the line on the graph is horizontal.

## 2 Discussing Graphs of Speed

You may use the following discussion questions to review the investigation and give students more familiarity with speed-time graphs.

- What does a speed-time graph of constant speed look like?

- On Graph D, do you think the speed during each 1-hour interval was exactly constant? Why or why not? (Answer: No. Realistically speed changes as the car speeds up and slows down, especially as it starts and stops, so the speeds shown must be averages.)

**72A** **MATHEMATICS OF MOTION** • LESSON 10

Problem Solving

1) Graph A shows how far the Lin family is away from home at each time. Graph B shows how hungry the Lins are on their trip because they are most hungry right before. Graph C shows the total distance the Lins have drove. Graph D is the Lins speed in m.p.h. on their trip.

A → label axis as distance or miles.

 → label axis as hunger

 → label axis as distance or miles.

 → label axis as speed (m.p.h.)

 → scale should be 10 miles for each slot.

 → scale should be hunger level or strength on a scale of 1 to 5

 → scale should be 20 miles for each slot.

 → scale should be 10 m.p.h. for each slot.

# 10 How Fast? How Far? How Long?

EXPLORING
SPEED-TIME
GRAPHS

**Study the graphs in this lesson carefully.** They contain information that you have not seen in a graph before. Your job in the activities ahead is to learn how to create and interpret these new kinds of graphs.

## Problem Solve with New Kinds of Graphs

**What does each graph show?**

Read the story about the Lin's family trip. Then examine the four graphs of their trip and answer the following questions.

**1** What does each graph show?

**2** How should the vertical axis be labeled?

**3** What scale should go on the vertical axis?

### The Lins Go on an Outing

On Sunday, the Lin family set out on a car ride at 10 A.M. For the first hour, they drove at a speed of 40 miles per hour. In the second hour, traffic was heavy, so they only drove at 20 miles per hour. From 12 P.M. to 1 P.M., they stopped for lunch and did not drive at all. After lunch, it started to rain, so they decided to go home. They drove at 30 miles per hour to get home.

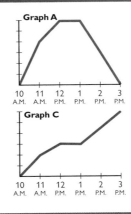

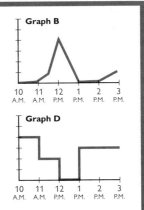

*We answered the follow-up questions with a 20-questions format. The class had 20 questions to figure out what motion was graphed, but each question had to be answered only "yes" or "no." There were lots of surprises as the class uncovered the mystery of each pair of graphs.* □

*My students played "Guess the Motion" with their graphs from the investigation. They covered up any give-away words on their graphs and had their partners guess what motion the graph represented. Hints, such as estimated average speed, whether the graph depicts an athletic event, an animal moving, and so on, were allowed.* □

*I had all my students who graphed the same or similar motions get in groups to compare their graphs and write a paper summarizing the similarities and differences among their graphs.* □

*student page*

## 3 Creating Distance-Time and Speed-Time Graphs

Some students may understand quickly how to make speed-time graphs, from their understanding of distance-time graphs. Others may need help thinking about what scales to use, how to label the axes, and how to show something speeding up or slowing down on the graph. This is a good opportunity for students to work together to figure out how to make this new type of graph. Groups of three will work well.

## 4 Sharing and Discussing: What's the Motion?

Ask students to cover up any words on their graphs that tell what moved. Then have them take turns showing their two graphs of a motion and seeing if others can guess what motion was graphed. If needed, average speed, top speed, whether the graph shows an athletic event or animal moving, or other hints can be given. Look for opportunities to discuss the following questions.

- Do we have any examples of very different motions having graphs that look very similar in shape (if we don't consider the scales)? For example, does a speed-time graph of an airplane taking off look at all like a speed-time graph of someone skiing down a hill?

- How did you find or estimate the average speed and the fastest speed? How could you check that the graphs show these correctly?

*student page*

## 5 Deciding Which Graph to Use

Some of the questions can be answered with information from any of the graphs (e.g., how much time was spent traveling), some can be answered more easily from one type of graph (e.g., when one person is moving twice as fast as another), and some cannot be answered by any of the graphs (e.g., when two people are moving in opposite directions).

Be sure all students are clear on the three types of graphs they are considering:

- Distance-time A: shows distance from starting point over time.

- Distance-time B: shows total distance traveled over time.

- Speed-time: shows average speed during each time interval.

- narratives indicating that flat sections of a graph mean that whatever is being graphed is not changing?
- speed-time graphs that feature correctly scaled and labeled axes, and show objects speeding up and slowing down correctly?
- a definite method to estimate fastest speed and average speed?

See *Mathematics of Motion* Assessment page A13 for assessment information.

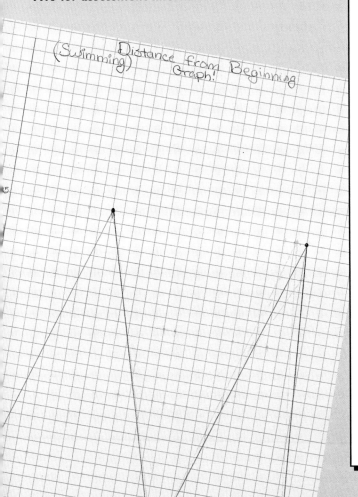

(Swimming) Distance from Beginning Graph!

## Create Distance-Time and Speed-Time Graphs

**What do the graphs of some familiar motions look like?**

**1** Choose three different motions you have done or seen. Here are some motions you could use, or you can think up your own.

a. someone going down a water slide

b. someone on a bicycle climbing to the top of a hill and then coasting down the other side

c. the movement of a child in a swing

d. an airplane taking off

e. someone who jumps out of an airplane and opens her parachute when halfway down

f. an athlete in the high-jump event at the Olympics

g. a baseball being pitched and then hit for a home run

h. a cat trying to catch a mouse

**2** For each motion, create one type of distance-time graph and a speed-time graph.

**3** For each motion, also find or estimate the average speed and the fastest speed reached during the motion. When was the person, animal, or object moving the fastest?

## Decide Which Graph to Use

Consider the three types of graphs about motions. For each question, say which graph or graphs you would use to find the information you need, and how you would find it. Questions 3, 4, and 5 are for graphs that show more than one person moving.

### Information from Graphs of Motion

1. How far did someone travel?

2. How much time did someone spend traveling?

3. Who is traveling the fastest?

4. Is one person moving twice as fast as another?

5. When are two people moving in opposite directions?

6. What is someone's average speed over a whole trip?

*hot* **words** | slope
speed-time graph

**H W omework**

page 87

# LESSON 11

## Solving Distance, Speed, and Time Problems

*Several of my students were surprised to find that some calculated answers did not match their graphs. For example, in problem 1, they assumed that since half the total distance was covered at 60 mph and the other half at 30 mph, the average speed would be 45 mph. But their distance-time graphs showed that the total distance of 120 miles was covered in 3 hours, for an average speed of 40 miles per hour. More time was spent driving at 30 mph than at 60 mph, so simply averaging the two speeds didn't give the correct answer.* □

*I had my students do the homework assignment on distance, speed, and time problems in class. I was able to give them extra support while they were working with the equations for the first time.* □

# The Race Is On!

student page

## 1 Problem Solving with Average Speed

Begin by asking students the following questions.

- The world record for women in the 100-meter race is 10.5 seconds—about 10 meters per second. The marathon is more than 42,000 meters, or more than 420 times as long as the 100-meter race. What average speed per second would you predict for the women's record marathon?

- What average speed per second would you predict for the women's record 1,500-meter run?

After students give their estimates, have them begin work on the World Record Times problems. In order to compare speeds, students will need to express the speeds for all the races in the same units, such as meters per second.

(Answers: 1. 100 m: 9.524 m/sec; 200 m: 9.4 m/sec; 400 m: 8.403 m/sec; 800 m: 7.080 m/sec; 1,500 m: 6.494 m/sec; 3,000 m: 6.173 m/sec; 10,000 m: 5.643 m/sec; marathon: 5.211 m/sec 2. Average speed slows as distance increases. 3. Predictions will vary.)

Next, ask students to state the distance equation and provide its rearranged forms. Then formally state the equation and its three possible arrangements.

- $d = s \times t$ (total distance = average speed × total time)

- $s = d \div t$ (average speed = total distance ÷ total time)

- $t = d \div s$ (total time = total distance ÷ average speed)

Distribute one copy of Distance, Speed, and Time Problems, Reproducible R16, to each student. You may want students to work in pairs to complete the problems on the page and make graphs to check their work. Discuss solutions in class. For additional practice, you may use the following examples. The homework for this lesson provides additional practice problems.

- What is the average speed of a cheetah that sprints 100 meters in 4 seconds? that sprints 50 meters in 2 seconds? (Answers: 25 m/sec; 25 m/sec)

- If a car moves with an average speed of 60 km/hr for an hour, it will travel a distance of 60 km. How far would it travel at this rate in 4 hours? in 10 hours? (Answers: 240 km; 600 km)

- How long does it take a tree to grow 2.4 meters if it grows at a rate of 0.8 m/yr? If it grows 12 cm/yr? (Answers: 3 yr; 20 yr)

# homework options

**LESSON HOMEWORK**

*Page 88*

*hot* **topics**

- *Evaluating Expressions and Formulas (6•3)*
  *Exercises 1–4, 8–10*

## Distance, Speed, and Time Problems

Solve each of the following problems using the following equations. Then create a graph that you can use to check and show that your answer is correct. Be careful; some of these problems are tricky!

$d = s \times t$ (total distance = average speed × total time)
$s = d \div t$ (average speed = total distance ÷ total time)
$t = d \div s$ (total time = total distance ÷ average speed)

**1. What is the average speed?**

We drove 60 miles to visit our friends' new baby. Then we drove 60 miles to get back home. On the way there, we drove at a speed of 60 miles per hour. On the way back, we drove at a speed of 30 miles per hour. What was our average speed for the whole trip?

*[handwritten]* $s = d \div t$  $d = 60 + 60 = 120$ miles  way there = 1 hr  way back = 2 hrs
$s = \dfrac{120\,mi}{3\,hrs} = \boxed{40\ mph}$

**2. Who won the race?**

In a bicycle race of 10 miles, Rachel gave Simone a head start of 2 miles. Simone rode at an average speed of 20 miles per hour. Rachel rode at an average speed of 25 miles per hour. Who won the race?

*[handwritten]* $t = d \div s$  Rachel's time $= \dfrac{10\,mi}{25\,mph} = 0.4\,h$  Simone's $= 8\,mi$
time $= \dfrac{20\,mph}{}$  $= 0.4\,h$
$\boxed{\text{The race is a tie}}$

**Click and Clack's trip**

Click and Clack took a trip. The table below shows how long they traveled at each speed. How far did they travel during the whole trip? $1.667 + 6.667 + 15 + 26.667 = \boxed{50.001\ \text{km}}$
How far did they travel at each speed?
What was their average speed for the trip? $s = d \div t = 50,001\ km \div (10+20+30+40) = \dfrac{50,001 \div 100}{} = 0.50\ km/min$
$= 50,001 \div 100$

| They Traveled at This Speed | For This Amount of Time |
|---|---|
| 10 kilometers per hour | 10 minutes |
| 20 kilometers per hour | 20 minutes |
| 30 kilometers per hour | 30 minutes |
| 40 kilometers per hour | 40 minutes |

*[handwritten]* HOW FAR
$10\,km/hr \times \tfrac{1}{6}\,hr = 1.667\,km$
$20\,km/hr \times \tfrac{1}{3}\,hr = 6.667\,km$
$30\,km/hr \times \tfrac{1}{2}\,hr = 15\,km$
$40\,km/hr \times \tfrac{2}{3}\,hr = 26.667\,km$
$\boxed{\dfrac{30\ km}{hr}}$

---

# 11 The Race Is On!

**SOLVING DISTANCE, SPEED, AND TIME PROBLEMS**

**Most things don't move with constant speed.** Take your bike, for example. You start off slowly, pedal to a coasting speed, slow down soon and pedal again. Constant speed is rare. So in problem solving, you often use average speed.

## Problem Solve with Average Speed

**What equations relate distance, speed, and time?**

Use the table to answer the following questions.

**1** For each distance, what is the average speed of the world champion runner?

**2** How does the average speed change as the distance of the race increases?

**3** What average speed would you predict as the world record for the following women's races:

  **a.** 1,000 meter    **b.** 5,000 meter    **c.** 25,000 meter

### World's Running Records for Women

| Distance | Time | Runner and Year |
|---|---|---|
| 100 meters | 10.5 seconds | Florence Griffith-Joyner, 1988 |
| 200 meters | 21.3 seconds | Florence Griffith-Joyner, 1988 |
| 400 meters | 47.6 seconds | Marita Koch, 1985 |
| 800 meters | 1 minute, 53 seconds | J. Kratochvilova, 1983 |
| 1,500 meters | 3 minutes, 51 seconds | Qu Yunxia, 1993 |
| 3,000 meters | 8 minutes, 6 seconds | Wang Junxia, 1993 |
| 10,000 meters | 29 minutes, 32 seconds | Wang Junxia, 1993 |
| 42,206 meters (marathon) | 2 hours, 15 minutes | Paula Radcliffe, 2003 |

*I suggested that students get together with partners to brainstorm story ideas. They came up with lots of interesting topics, including a snowmobile race, a race between three babies, three children rollerblading, and a tourist stumbling across a farmer and his cow. □*

*We started this activity by discussing an example together as a class. I suggested that the graph could be about a trip from Boston to New York. Since most of my students have visited friends and family in New York, this was familiar to them. We used their personal experiences to discuss how the labels on the axis and the events in the story would differ according to the mode of transportation. □*

*I had my students read their stories aloud to the class. I prepared a transparency of the graph, and as they read, I filled in the axis, and "traced" their stories on the graph. This helped students to assess their own and each other's stories. □*

## 2 ▸ Inventing the Story of a Graph

*student page*

Students are given a graph showing the pattern of motion of three unspecified movers—people, animals, or objects—over a time interval. Students set the distance and time scales, describe what is moving, and write a story consistent with the graph. They also create a total distance graph and a speed-time graph for the same movements. This problem can be used to assess students' learning of the material in this unit. If so, you may want to let students see the guidelines listed under the heading What To Look For in advance, so they will know how their work will be assessed.

Unless students are very familiar with graphing simultaneous motion from more than one starting point, you may want to spend a few minutes making sure they understand the positions of A, B, and C on the "Distance from" *y*-axis. Ask:

- Suppose A, B, and C are all students starting from home. What might zero represent? How will you fill in the label "Distance from ___"?

- Do you think any of students A, B, and C might go to the same place?

(Answers: While students' responses based on the graph on Student Guide page 75 will vary, they should each share some general characteristics.

1. A, B, and C all start at differing distances from a single location, which is zero on the graph and is included in the label for the *y*-axis. A has two periods of no change of distance—at the beginning and midway in the time period—and B has two periods of no change of distance—at the begin-

ning and end of the time. A and C move closer to the zero point, then away from it; B moves away, then back. It seems likely that B and C are in the same place, B's starting point, at the end of the time period.

2. Answers will vary.

3. B travels the least, A the next greatest, and C the greatest distance (no static periods).

4. The graph shows that C travels fastest at first, then at a similar speed to A. In the latter part of the time period, A travels fastest.

5. Average speeds should be calculated by dividing distance traveled by time in motion and stated in appropriate units.)

## 3 ▸ Reflecting on the Investigation

To help students think about what they learned and what they liked about the lesson, you can ask the following reflection questions. Students can answer them in writing, or use them for group discussion.

- What was the hardest part of this investigation?

- What part of the investigation did you feel most confident about?

- What questions do you have about the investigation?

- What things did you do during the lesson that you feel you would like more practice with?

- What was the most interesting idea you learned about in this lesson?

# what to look for

**DOES STUDENT WORK:**

- *use a distance scale and time scale appropriate for the story?*
- *describe movements for each character that are consistent with the graph?*
- *create a total distance graph consistent with the original graph?*
- *create a speed-time graph consistent with the original graph?*

**See *Mathematics of Motion* Assessment page A13 for assessment information.**

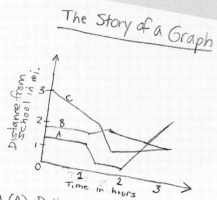

The Story of a Graph

STORY!
Adriana (A) Betty (B) and Carolyn (C) all are going to sell girl scout cookies around their neighborhood. They started at the same time. Each girl started at her own house at 1:00. Adriana and Betty took phone orders for one hour but Carolyn before leaving for one hour but Carolyn walked toward school. At 2:00 Betty walked away from school for ½ hour and Adrian went to houses closer to school for 20 minutes. At 2:20 Adrianna went to a house ere her friends lived and stayed there til 3:00. At 3:00 she sold cookies houses farther away from school. Betty rted walking away from school at 2:30 just about the time Carolyn started ing to houses closer to shool. Betty Carolyn met at the same house 4:00!

## Invent the Story of a Graph

The graph shows three people, animals, or objects (A, B, and C) that move over time. It shows their distances from a certain point.

**1** Write a story that goes with the graph. The story can be about anything you choose—people, animals, vehicles, or asteroids. Your story should include details about the speeds and directions of the three people, animals, or objects. Also say where the distances are measured from (zero on your graph).

**2** Decide on scales for the time and distance axes that match your story. Mark your scales on the graph.

**3** Draw a graph that shows the total distance traveled over the given time by A, B, and C. How far did each of A, B, and C travel?

**4** Draw a graph that shows the speeds at which each of A, B, and C traveled during your story.

**5** Find the average speed for each of A, B, and C.

What story will the graph tell when finished?

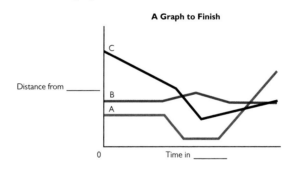

**A Graph to Finish**

Distance from _____

0        Time in _____

**hot words** | average speed
distance

**Homework**
page 88

# 12

## Combining Motion Data, Graphs, and Equations

*I wanted to show the class examples of student work that demonstrated fulfillment of my assessment criteria. Our physics teacher loaned me some lab reports having to do with the distance equation. The reports provided examples of graphs, data display, and data analysis that were clear and informative. Next year, I'll show examples of this year's final projects, so students can see how they were assessed.* □

*I asked my students to do a thumbnail sketch of their projects for my approval. Students included the motion they planned to investigate, how they planned to obtain data, and the kind of presentation they wanted to do. This helped them think in practical terms about what they could accomplish.* □

# Final Project

## 1 Planning the Project

There are three ways to use this final lesson.

- It could take two days for class presentations of final projects. In this case, students would be told about the project earlier in the unit and work on it outside of class.

- If students choose a topic and gather data outside of class, two days could be spent working on the project in class. In this case, students could exchange papers for feedback.

- Students could work on their projects outside of class and begin another unit in class. When projects are complete, they can be shared in class, taking a break from the new unit.

## 2 Discussing the Project and Assessment Criteria

Describe the final project so that everyone understands it before proceeding. You could also discuss assessment criteria such as the following.

- Does the student use a variety of methods (graphs, equations, stories, maps, etc.) to describe each motion?

- Does the student appropriately use vocabulary (e.g., average speed), units (e.g., feet per second), and tools (e.g., meterstick)?

- Are graphs, equations, stories, maps, and so on, correct and consistent with each other and consistent with the collected data?

- Does the student make useful and correct comparisons between the people/objects that were studied?

- Is the presentation of results clear and interesting?

## 3 Collecting the Motion Data

Encourage students to choose a situation for which extensive data is available or for which actual data can be collected. They should gather as much data as possible about intermediate times, distances, and speeds. For example, knowing the winning time of the Indy 500 allows students to calculate average speed, but times for intermediate marks give students the option of presenting a more thorough description of the race.

Be sure students choose a type of motion that allows for a comparison between at least two people, animals, or objects. You may wish to check their ideas before they begin.

# homework options

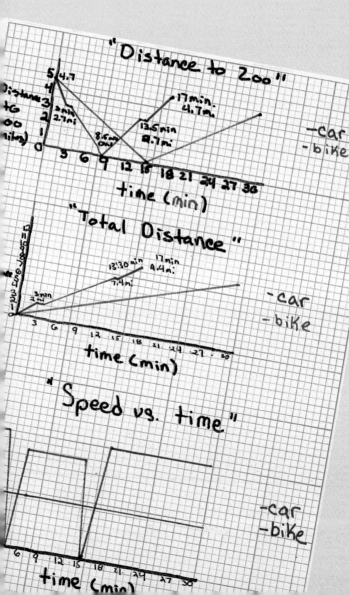

# 12 Final Project

COMBINING MOTION
DATA, GRAPHS, AND
EQUATIONS

**Here is your chance to use everything you have learned about motion to analyze, compare, and describe motions of your own choosing.**

## Collect the Motion Data

**What kind of motion should you study?**

Gather data about a motion of your own choosing.

**1** Pick a situation from Sample Motions that allows you to compare the motion of two or more people, animals, or objects.

**2** Collect as much data on the motion as you can. For each of the people or objects you will be comparing, be sure to find as many times, speeds, and distances as possible.

### Sample Motions

- An express train and a local train that pass through your town

- The winner of the Indy 500 and the driver who came in second

- The results of two participants in your school's 100-meter race

- Olympic track and field events, such as the 100-meter sprint, the hurdles, the long jump, or the high jump

- Walking and rollerblading

- Flying from Atlanta to Los Angeles on an airplane versus taking a train

- A jaguar and a cheetah

- A jaguar and a tortoise

- The speed of a hockey puck versus the speed of a baseball

- Balls rolling down ramps with different slopes

- Bicycling in different gears

*The students really got involved in their final projects. There were a number of fabulous ones! Leslie did a multimedia presentation complete with music. Another student, Ron, prepared a comic book based on his story comparing the motions of a safari adventurer and the lion that pursued him. Several students made posters that I displayed on the wall for several days. □*

*To my delight, most of my students wanted to present their projects to the class. There was so much enthusiasm that I allowed 5 minutes for each student to show his or her work. To keep those in the audience on task, I had them take notes that stated the main strengths of one another's presentations. □*

*One of the reasons the final project was so successful with my group was that it allowed students to express their individuality and use their own learning styles while still utilizing the math skills they learned in the unit. □*

*student page*

## 4 Analyzing the Motion

Remind students to analyze their data in as many ways as possible. For example, a student who has recorded that a local train takes 8 minutes to travel between towns that are 4 miles apart should find an average speed of 30 mi/hr. This can be extended to an equation, $d = 30t$, where $d$ is distance in miles and $t$ is time in hours. This equation can be graphed on a coordinate grid that also shows a faster express train.

Encourage students to use their equations and graphs to make predictions of times and distances that were not included in the initial data.

*student page*

## 5 Describing and Displaying the Motion

Have students compile and display their results in charts, booklets, or other formats. Remind them that they should display their results clearly and demonstrate their knowledge of the main concepts of this unit.

You may want to have students work on this aspect of their projects in teams of 2–4, so that they can brainstorm presentation ideas, share insights, and revise their work accordingly.

## 6 Assessing the Projects

Before assessing the projects, you might ask students to assess each other's work, if time permits. This can be done in several ways: students can share projects in pairs or small groups, or some or all of them can present their projects to the entire class. Remind students to assess each other's work constructively, using the criteria developed in Step 1. You may also want to give students a chance to revise their work based on peer feedback before turning in their projects.

# assessment criteria

**DO STUDENTS' FINAL PROJECTS:**

• *apply the distance equation to calculate average speed and solve problems using real-world data?*

• *create distance-from, distance-to, total distance, and speed-time graphs to represent motion?*

• *represent motion using various means including stories, graphs, and maps?*

• *distinguish between average speed and peak speed and apply both concepts to analyze motion?*

**See *Mathematics of Motion* Assessment pages A14–A15 for assessment information.**

# ADDITIONAL assessment
O p t i o n s

• **Assessment Rubric,** page A15

• **Phase Three Student Assessment Criteria,** page R5

• **Phase Three Skill Quiz,** page R4

• **Phase Three Skill Quiz Answers,** page A16

## Analyze the Motion

For each of the people or objects that you are comparing, analyze the data you collected and determine each of the following.

- the total distance traveled and the total time

- the average speed over the entire trip

- intermediate speeds, whenever possible

- equations that can be used to calculate time, speed, and/or distance for each person/object

- graphs displaying total distance traveled, distance from a starting point, and speed versus time

- graphs that compare the motion of the two people/objects

## Describe and Display the Motion

Prepare a chart, booklet, or other presentation that describes and displays your findings as fully as possible. Be sure to include the following:

- your initial data about the motion

- all of the equations you developed

- graphs of all motions

- maps, diagrams, or illustrations describing each motion

- written descriptions or stories for each motion

Your final project should show how much you know about motion.

*hot* **words** | total distance (formula $d = s \times t$)
statistics

**H**omework

page 89

# Moving, Measuring, and Representing

## Applying Skills

For each motion, tell which of these speeds are possible: 200 meters per second, 27 feet per second, 20 miles per hour, 90 feet per second, 50 meters per hour, 500 miles per hour, 300 feet per second, 5 feet per hour.

**1.** a jet plane flying

**2.** a cheetah running at full speed

**3.** an athlete sprinting

**4.** a snail crawling

**What units could you use for each motion?**

**5.** a train traveling at full speed

**6.** the turning of a phonograph record

**7.** the rotation of the hour hand of a clock

**8.** a spider walking on a wall

## Extending Concepts

**9.** Use the second hand of your watch to measure your pulse rate for 1 minute. Give the rate together with the appropriate units.

**10.** Find a space where you can walk for 10 seconds. Walk at your normal pace for 10 seconds and count how many steps you take. Estimate your stride length in feet. Estimate the distance that you would cover in 1 minute. Estimate your walking speed in feet per minute.

## Making Connections

A *tsunami* (tidal wave) may be caused by an earthquake beneath the ocean. Its speed depends on the depth of the ocean. As it approaches shallow water along a coast, it slows and may increase in height to as much as 115 ft. Each picture below gives information about a tsunami.

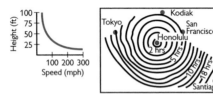

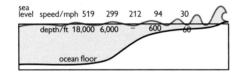

**11.** What information is given in each representation? For each one, give an example of a question that could be answered using that representation.

**12.** Which representation, if any, would you use to answer the question, "How fast was the tsunami traveling when it was 500 miles from Hawaii?" Explain.

**13.** Write three questions about tsunamis that cannot be answered using any of the representations above.

## Homework

### Solutions: Lesson 1

1. 200 m/sec, 500 mph
2. 90 ft/sec
3. 27 ft/sec, 20 mph
4. 5 ft/hr

Answers 5–8 may vary. Possible answers:

5. miles per hour
6. revolutions per minute
7. degrees per hour
8. feet per minute

Answers 9–10 will vary.

9. Appropriate units are beats per minute.
10. Answers will vary. Typical walking speeds are around 300 ft/min.
11. Questions will vary. The following information is given by the three representations:
    i. how the height of a tsunami varies with its speed
    ii. the time it will take for the tsunami to reach different cities
    iii. how the speed of a tsunami varies with the depth of the ocean
12. None of the representations can be used.
13. Answers will vary.

## Solutions: Lesson 2

**1–3.** Answers will vary.

**4.** Column 1: 5 ft; 300 ft; 18,000 ft or 3.41 mi; 1,056 sec or 17 min, 36 sec; Column 2: 8.5 ft; 510 ft; 30,600 ft or 5.80 mi; 621 sec or 10 min, 21 sec; Column 3: 28 ft; 1,680 ft; 100,800 ft or 19.09 mi; 188.6 sec or 3 min, 8.6 sec

**5.** 2.5 hr; 48 ft; 40 m/min

**6. a.** 1,400 ft; 84,000 ft or 15.91 mi; 15.91 mph

   **b.** Assumed that he would continue to run at the same pace; no; he would be unable to maintain that pace over a longer distance and would slow down; estimates will vary.

**7. a.** 20 sec; 5 sec

   **b.** Her speed is the same as Daniel's.

   **c.** His speed is four times Daniel's speed.

**8. a.** About 669,600,000 mi; about 669,600,000 mph

   **b.** 36,500 ft or 6.91 mi; 4.17 ft; 0.000789 mph

# Going the Distance

### Applying Skills

Estimate how far you would go in 20 seconds by:

**1.** walking quickly

**2.** hopping

**3.** walking backward

**4.** Copy and complete the table below.

| | Walking | Jogging | Cycling |
|---|---|---|---|
| Distance in 10 seconds | 50 feet | 85 feet | 280 feet |
| Distance in 1 second | | | |
| Distance in 1 minute | | | |
| Distance in 1 hour | | | |
| Time to go 1 mile | | | |

**5.** Copy and complete the table below. Include the appropriate units.

| Distance | Time | Speed |
|---|---|---|
| 100 miles | | 40 miles per hour |
| | 8 seconds | 6 feet per second |
| 160 meters | 4 minutes | |

### Extending Concepts

**6. a.** Bill runs as fast as he can for 12 seconds and covers a distance of 280 feet. At that pace, how far would he run in one minute? in one hour? What is his speed in miles per hour?

   **b.** In item **6a**, when you calculated how far Bill would run in one hour, what assumption did you make? Do you think he would really run that far in an hour? Why or why not? How far do you think he would run?

**7.** Daniel runs the length of his backyard in 10 seconds.

   **a.** If Scott runs the length of the yard at half Daniel's speed, how long will it take him? How long will it take him at twice Daniel's speed?

   **b.** If Kemi runs three times the length of the yard in 30 seconds, how does her speed compare to Daniel's?

   **c.** If Doug runs twice the length of the yard in 5 seconds, how does his speed compare to Daniel's speed?

### Making Connections

**8. a.** The speed of light in a vacuum is about 186,000 miles per second. How far would light travel in a vacuum in one hour? What is its speed in miles per hour?

   **b.** The speed of a glacier depends on its steepness and its temperature. A steep, warm glacier may flow as much as 100 feet per day. At this rate, how far would it flow in a year? in one hour? What would its speed be in miles per hour?

# Reporting Live from the Parade

### Applying Skills

The field notes below give information about the position of characters in a parade. Use this and your Snapshot Sequence Sheets to answer the questions. The distance between each pair of landmarks on your Snapshot Sequence Sheet is 15 meters.

| | |
|---|---|
| **A** | = Acrobat |
| **AD** | = African Drummers |
| **CT** | = Capoeira Troupe |

**1st Snapshot, 10:30:00 A.M.**
A:   At Gas Station
AD: 10 meters past Gas Station
CT:  At Taco Zone

**2nd Snapshot, 10:30:10 A.M.**
A:   5 meters past Dog Lovers' Club
AD: 5 meters past Dog Lovers' Club
CT:  At Taco Zone

**3rd Snapshot, 10:30:20 A.M.**
A:   10 meters past Taco Zone
AD: At Taco Zone
CT:  At Taco Zone

**4th Snapshot, 10:30:30 A.M.**
A:   At *U.F.O. Chronicle*
AD: 10 meters past Taco Zone
CT:  At Taco Zone

**1.** Use the field notes to complete the first four pictures of your Snapshot Sequence Sheet. In each picture, record the positions of the characters.

**2.** How far is it from the Taco Zone to the T-Shirt Hut? from the TreeWatch booth to the stop sign at Avenue B?

**3.** How much time is there between consecutive snapshots?

**4.** How much time is represented by Snapshots 1–4 all together?

**5.** How far does each character travel between snapshots?

**6.** How fast, in meters per second, is each character moving? Who is traveling the fastest?

### Extending Concepts

**7.** Write a rule you can use to calculate how far in meters the acrobat would move in any given number of minutes. Use *D* to stand for the distance and *M* for the number of minutes. Use your rule to figure out how far the acrobat would move in 9 minutes.

**8.** Write a rule you can use to calculate how many snapshots would be taken in any given number of minutes. Use *P* to stand for the number of snapshots and *M* for the number of minutes. How many snapshots would be taken in 9 minutes?

**9.** Write your own snapshot sequence for Snapshots 5–8 to show how the parade characters might continue. Use your sequence to complete Pictures 5–8 of your Snapshot Sequence Sheet.

### Writing

**10.** Write a short narrative describing what the three parade characters might have been doing in Snapshots 1–8. Explain how you can tell.

**Solutions: Lesson 3**

1. Check students' Snapshot Sequence Sheets.
2. 45 m; 45 m from the TreeWatch booth to the stop sign at Avenue B
3. 10 sec
4. 30 sec
5. Acrobat: 20 m; African Drummers: 10 m; Capoeira Troupe: 0 m
6. Acrobat: 2 m/sec; African Drummers: 1 m/sec; Capoeira Troupe: 0 m/sec; the acrobat
7. $D = 120M$; 1,080 m
8. $P = 6M$; 54
9. Answers will vary.
10. Answers will vary.

## Solutions: Lesson 4

1. Check students' Snapshot Sequence Sheets.

2. Check students' Snapshot Sequence Sheets. Snapshot 3 should show: SW: at TreeWatch; S: 10 m past Tree-Watch; D: 10 m past Dog Lovers' Club

   Snapshot 4 should show: SW: at Taco Zone; S: at *U.F.O. Chronicle*; D: 5 m past Taco Zone

3. Stilt walker: 3 m/sec toward Avenue A; Saxophonist: 1 m/sec toward Avenue B; Danny: 2 m/sec toward Avenue B

4. Stilt walker: 900 m; Saxophonist: 300 m; Danny: 600 m

5. 2:20:10: Stilt walker: at TreeWatch; Saxophonist: 10 m past TreeWatch; Danny: 10 m past Dog Lover's Club

   2:20:11: Stilt walker: 3 m below TreeWatch; Saxophonist: 11 m past TreeWatch; Danny: 12 m past Dog Lover's Club

   2:20:12: Stilt walker: 6 m below TreeWatch; Saxophonist: 12 m past TreeWatch; Danny: 14 m past Dog Lover's Club

   2:20:13: Stilt walker: 9 m below TreeWatch; Saxophonist: 13 m past TreeWatch; Danny: 1 m past Taco Zone

   2:20:14: Stilt walker: 12 m below TreeWatch; Saxophonist: 14 m past TreeWatch; Danny: 3 m past Taco Zone

   2:20:15: Stilt walker: at Taco Zone; Saxophonist: at *U.F.O. Chronicle*; Danny: 5 m past Taco Zone; Danny and the stilt walker pass at 2:20:14

6. a. Find distance moved between snapshots and time between snapshots; divide distance by time.

   b. Compare the steepness of lines showing the paths of the two characters or objects: the steeper the line, the faster the motion.

   c. Use the snapshots to find the speed of the character as described in item **6a**. Assume that the character moved at constant speed between snapshots and calculate distance moved in each smaller time period by multiplying speed by time.

7. Answers will vary.

---

# The Parade Continues

**Homework 4**

### Applying Skills

The field notes below give information about the position of characters in a parade. Use this and your Snapshot Sequence Sheet to answer the questions. The distance between each pair of landmarks on your Snapshot Sequence Sheet is 15 meters.

---

**SW** = Stilt Walker, **S** = Saxophonist, **D** = Danny

**1st Snapshot, 2:20:00 P.M.**
SW: At T-Shirt Hut
S:   At TreeWatch
D:   5 meters past Gas Station

**2nd Snapshot, 2:20:05 P.M.**
SW: At *U.F.O. Chronicle*
S:   5 meters past TreeWatch
D:   At Dog Lovers' Club

**3rd and 4th Snapshots**
Too cloudy

**5th Snapshot, 2:20:20 P.M.**
SW: At Dog Lovers' Club
S:   5 meters past *U.F.O. Chronicle*
D:   At TreeWatch

---

1. Use the field notes to complete Pictures 1, 2, and 5 of your Snapshot Sequence Sheet. In each picture, record the positions of the characters.

2. Figure out what the 3rd and 4th pictures would have looked like and complete Pictures 3 and 4 of your Snapshot Sequence Sheet.

3. Find the speed and direction of each character.

4. How far would each character travel in 5 minutes?

### Extending Concepts

5. What happened between 2:20:10 and 2:20:15? Create a snapshot sequence with a picture every 1 second between 2:20:10 and 2:20:15. At what point did Danny and the stilt walker pass?

6. Explain how you can use a snapshot sequence to figure out:

   a. the speed at which an object is traveling

   b. when one object is traveling faster than another

   c. what probably happened between two snapshots

### Writing

7. Write a story explaining the following snapshot sequence. Explain who the characters are and what is at each marker along the road. Give the distance between markers and time between snapshots. Give the speeds and directions of the characters. Explain why they are moving that way.

| Picture | 1 | 2 | 3 | 4 |
|---|---|---|---|---|
| Time | | | | |

# Walk This Way

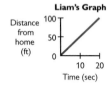 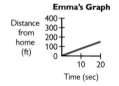

## Applying Skills

Mary walked 200 feet along a straight line in 40 seconds. Follow the guidelines to make a distance-time graph.

**1.** Draw axes for a graph. Label the horizontal axis "Time (seconds)" and the vertical axis "Distance from starting point (feet)."

**2.** Set the scale for each axis. Mark equal divisions along each axis.

**3.** How long did it take her to walk the entire distance? Mark that point.

**4.** Assuming that Mary's speed was constant, how long did it take her to walk half the distance? Mark that point.

**5.** Draw the line showing the entire walk.

## Extending Concepts

The graphs for items **6–9** all represent motion along a straight line.

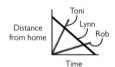

**6.** In Toni, Lynn, and Rob's graph, who walked the fastest? the slowest? How can you tell?

**7.** Why does Lynn's graph slope downward?

**Liam's Graph**     **Emma's Graph**

**8.** How far did Liam and Emma walk in 20 seconds? Who walked faster? Whose graph looks steeper? Why is it not true in this case that a steeper graph indicates a faster motion?

**9.** Which graph, Liam's or Emma's, has a more suitable scale? Why?

Tyler set out from the trailhead at 9:00 A.M. He walked for 1 hour, going 3 miles, and then rested for 20 minutes. He continued a little more slowly and reached Mirror Lake at 12:20 P.M. Suzi left the trailhead at 10:00 A.M. She walked steadily without breaks and also reached the lake at 12:20 P.M.

**10.** Create a graph to show what happens in the above story. Be sure to show the distances and times for each person. Estimate how far each person walked. Assume that each person walks along a straight line.

## Making Connections

**11.** The Pronghorn antelope is the swiftest North American mammal. It can run 200 meters in about 7.5 seconds. The fastest human can run 200 meters in about 20 seconds. Using the same axes, make distance-time graphs for a Pronghorn antelope and a human.

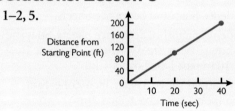

## Solutions: Lesson 5

**1–2, 5.**

**3.** 40 sec            **4.** 20 sec

**6.** Toni; Rob; The line for Toni is steeper than the line for Rob.

**7.** Her distance from home was decreasing.

**8.** Liam: 100 ft; Emma: 150 ft; Emma; Liam's; The scales are different.

**9.** Liam's; The distance scale is more "spread out," which makes it easier to read accurately.

**10.** Answers may vary. Possible answer:

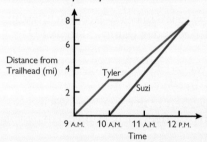

Estimates of distance each person walked should be around 8 miles.

**11.**

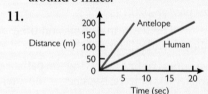

## Solutions: Lesson 6

1. 6:35 P.M.; approximate; graph
2. 4; exact; map
3. for his sister's birthday; story
4. Between 5:45 and 5:55 P.M.; between 5:40 and 5:45 P.M. and between 5:55 and 6:05 P.M. he wasn't moving at all; graph; approximate
5. to reach the store before it closed; story
6. 5 minutes; graph; approximate
7. east; map; exact
8. 6:05 P.M.–6:35 P.M.; graph; approximate
9. Answers will vary.
10. Answers will vary.

# Stories, Maps, and Graphs

### Applying Skills

Use the story, map, and graph below to answer the questions. Tell whether each answer is exact or approximate and whether you used the story and map below or graph in column 2 to find it.

It was Friday evening. David remembered that his sister's birthday was the next day. He decided to buy her a CD. He left his house on Hill Street at 5:30 P.M. to walk to the store. A few moments later, he ran into a friend and stopped to chat for a while. When he left his friend, he remembered that the CD store would close at 6:00 P.M., and he ran the rest of the way. He reached the store in time, bought a CD, and walked home.

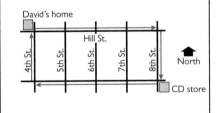

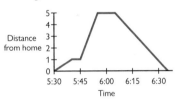

1. At what time did David return home?

2. How many blocks did David walk along Hill Street before turning?

3. Why did David want to buy a CD?

4. When was David traveling the fastest? the slowest?

5. Why did David hurry as he left his friend?

6. How long did David spend talking to his friend?

7. In what direction was David traveling when he first left his house?

8. During what time period(s) was David moving closer to his house?

### Extending Concepts

9. Write a story to describe a fantasy trip. Make a map and a distance-time graph to go with your story. Then make a second graph showing how a character in your story felt during the trip.

### Writing

10. Make up a question about your story that can be answered most easily using your map. Make up another question that can be answered most easily using your distance-time graph.

# A Graphing Matter

## Applying Skills

John walked 100 feet in a straight line from the starting point to the ending point in 15 seconds, then 40 feet back toward the starting point in 5 seconds. He waited 5 seconds, then walked all the way back to the start in 10 seconds. His "Distance from Start" graph is shown here.

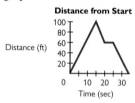

**Distance from Start**

Follow the guidelines to make John's "Distance to End Point" graph.

**1.** Draw axes for a graph. Label each axis appropriately. Set the scale.

**2.** Find John's distance to the ending point after 0, 15, 20, 25, and 35 seconds. Mark those points. Draw the line showing the entire walk.

Follow the guidelines to make John's "Total Distance" graph.

**3.** Draw axes for a graph. Label each axis appropriately. What is the total distance that John walked? What will be the largest number on the vertical axis? Set the scale on each axis.

**4.** Find the total distance John had walked after 0, 15, 20, 25, and 35 seconds. Mark those points. Draw the line showing the entire walk.

## Extending Concepts

**5.** The three graphs at right show total distance, distance to ending point, and distance from starting point. Which is which? How can you tell?

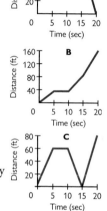

**6.** Which two graphs could represent the same motion? For each pair of graphs that could *not* represent the same motion, explain why not.

## Making Connections

The gray whale migrates seasonally between its breeding ground in Baja California and its feeding ground in the Arctic. The graph shows distance to the Arctic for the gray whale for a one-year period.

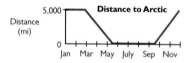

**Distance to Arctic**

**7.** A part of the graph is sloped upward. What are the whales doing during this time period? Where are they during February? How can you tell?

**8.** Draw the corresponding "Distance from Baja" and "Total Distance" graphs. Explain how you figured them out.

---

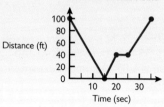

## Solutions: Lesson 7

**1–2.**

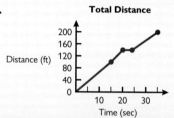

**Distance to End Point**

**3–4.**

**Total Distance**

**5.** A: distance to ending point, B: total distance, C: distance from starting point; For A, the distance after 20 sec is 0 ft; for B, the distance never decreases as time increases; for C, the distance at 0 sec is 0 ft.

**6.** A and B could represent the same motion.

**7.** Migrating from the Arctic to Baja California; Baja California; Their distance from the Arctic is 5,000 mi in February.

**8.**

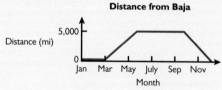

**Distance from Baja**

**Total Distance**

## Solutions: Lesson 8

1. a, d; They never show a decrease in distance as time increases.

2. c

3. a, b, d

4. Check students' graphs. Graphs should never show a decrease in distance.

5. time; distance; no        6. 4 mi

7. He was not moving.

8. Initially, her distance from home was increasing; later, it was decreasing.

9. No; we know only the total distance he traveled, not the direction he traveled in; at home

10. They could not have walked home together—Leah walked faster than Jamie between 1 and 2 P.M.

11. Jamie could not have walked faster than Leah between 9 and 11 A.M., since both characters walked 4 miles in that 2-hr interval.

12. Leah could not have walked another mile north after lunch since she would then have been 5 miles from home. The graph shows that her maximum distance from home was 4 miles.

13. Answers will vary.

---

# Juan and Marina Go Walking

### Applying Skills

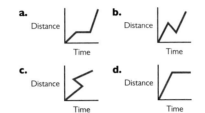

a. Distance / Time
b. Distance / Time
c. Distance / Time
d. Distance / Time

1. Which of the graphs above could show total distance traveled? Why?

2. Which graphs could not show the journey of a single person or vehicle?

3. Which graphs could represent distance from a point?

4. Sketch a distance-time graph that could show total distance traveled.

### Extending Concepts

**Leah's Graph**
**Distance (mi) from Home Against Time**

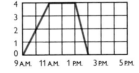

(y-axis: 0, 1, 2, 3, 4; x-axis: 9 A.M., 11 A.M., 1 P.M., 3 P.M., 5 P.M.)

**Jamie's Graph**
**Distance (mi) Walked Against Time**

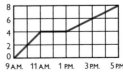

(y-axis: 2, 4, 6, 8; x-axis: 9 A.M., 11 A.M., 1 P.M., 3 P.M., 5 P.M.)

5. What is graphed on the horizontal axis of each graph shown? on the vertical axis? Are the scales of the two graphs the same?

6. How far did Jamie walk from 1 to 5 P.M.?

7. Why is there a flat portion on Jamie's graph between 11 A.M. and 1 P.M.?

8. Why does Leah's graph slope up and then down?

9. Can you tell where Jamie was at 5 P.M.? Why? Where was Leah at 2 P.M.?

**Explain why each story is inconsistent with the graphs in Extending Concepts.**

10. "Leah and Jamie left home at 9 A.M., walked together until 11 A.M., rested for two hours, and walked home together."

11. "Leah and Jamie left home at 9 A.M. Jamie walked faster than Leah until 11 A.M. Both rested between 11 A.M. and 1 P.M. Then they walked home."

12. "Leah and Jamie left home at 9 A.M. and walked 4 miles north. After lunch they walked another mile north. Then Jamie walked to his friend's house, and Leah walked home."

### Writing

13. Write your own imaginative story that matches the information on the two graphs in item **5** and the graph below. Use information from all three graphs.

**Jamie's Graph**
**How Tired Against Time**

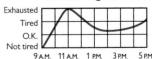

(y-axis: Exhausted, Tired, O.K., Not tired; x-axis: 9 A.M., 11 A.M., 1 P.M., 3 P.M., 5 P.M.)

# The Race Announcer

## Applying Skills

Refer to the graph of the running race for items 1–4.

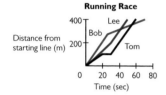

**Running Race**

Distance from starting line (m)

400 — Lee
Bob
200 — Tom
0  20  40  60  80
Time (sec)

1. At what times were there changes in speed?

2. At what time did Lee pass Bob?

3. What were the relative positions of the racers after 10 seconds?

4. How long did each person take to complete the race? Who won?

**Refer to the graph of the swimming race for items 5 and 6.**

5. Who is in the lead at 20 seconds? at 40 seconds? at 58 seconds? What is happening at 30 seconds?

6. How long does each person take to complete the first 30-meter lap? Who completes the first lap more quickly?

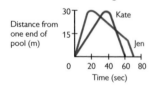

**Swimming Race**

Distance from one end of pool (m)

30 — Kate
15 — Jen
0  20  40  60  80
Time (sec)

## Extending Concepts

7. **a.** In the running race, what is the total distance that Tom runs? What is his total time? his average speed?

   **b.** What is Tom's speed at 10 seconds? 25 seconds? 40 seconds? Is there some point in the race when he was running at the average speed that you calculated in item **7a**? Explain.

   **c.** If you program a robot to roll at a constant speed in the race, at what speed should it roll to tie Tom? Draw a graph of the robot's race.

   **d.** Find Kate's average speed in the swimming race. How did you find it?

The report below doesn't give enough information to tell the final outcome. Draw two graphs that match the report but show different outcomes. Rewrite the report so that it fully and accurately describes one of your graphs.

8. "As they start on this 200-meter race, Sam is in the lead, Eric is behind him, then Raphael. Now, just 10 seconds into the race, Eric has tripped, and he's down. Raphael has passed him. This is amazing, with 50 meters to go Raphael passes Sam to win the race in 25 seconds."

## Writing

9. Use the graph in item **5** to write a commentary for the swimming race. Describe what is happening as fully and as accurately as you can.

**Solutions: Lesson 9**

1. Bob: at 25 sec; Lee: at 30 sec; Tom: at 20 sec and 30 sec
2. at about 40 sec
3. Bob in first place, Lee in second, Tom in third
4. Lee: 50 sec; Tom 60 sec; Bob 70 sec; Lee won
5. Jen; Jen; Kate; Jen and Kate pass each other moving in opposite directions.
6. Jen: 20 sec; Kate: 37 sec; Jen
7. **a.** 400 m; 60 sec; 6.7 m/sec
   **b.** 5 m/sec; 0 m/sec; 10 m/sec; no, 5 m/sec, 0 m/sec, and 10 m/sec are the only three speeds for Tom at any time during the race.
   **c.** 6.7 m/sec; check students' graphs
   **d.** 1 m/sec
8. Answers will vary. Check students' graphs. The report of the race fails to tell who came in second and how long it took the second and third runners to complete the race. Students should make one graph showing Eric in second place and another showing Sam in second place.
9. Answers will vary.

## Solutions: Lesson 10

1. distance-time graph; Amy: 12 mi; Brad: 40 mi

2. total distance or speed-time graph; Brad was traveling faster in each time period.

3. total distance graph; Amy: 7.5 mph; Brad: 25 mph

4. speed-time graph; Amy: 10 mph; Brad: 50 mph

5. speed-time graph; between 1:00 and 2:15 P.M.

6. total distance graph; Brad: 100 mi; Amy: 30 mi

7. 1:00–2:00 P.M.: 10 mph; 2:00–3:00 P.M.: 5 mph; 3:00–4:00 P.M.: 20 mph; 4:00–5:00 P.M.: 0 mph

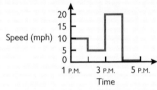

8. The speed is constant; a straight line; the speed is increasing. The speed-time graph in item 7 shows a constant speed within each time period. This is not realistic since speed is unlikely to stay exactly the same within each time period and because to change speeds from one time period to the next would take time. More realistically, the speed-time graph in item 7 shows the *average* speed within each time period.

9. a: speed is increasing at a constant rate; c: distance traveled increases at an increasing rate.

# How Fast? How Far? How Long?

### Applying Skills

For each question, tell which graph or graphs shown here could be used to find the information. Then answer the question.

1. How far was each person from home at 3:00 P.M.?

**Distance-Time Graph**

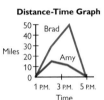

2. Who was traveling faster in each time period?

3. What was each person's average speed for the whole trip?

**Total Distance Graph**

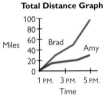

4. What was each person's exact speed at 4:30 P.M.?

5. During which time period(s) was Brad moving twice as fast as Amy?

**Speed-Time Graph**

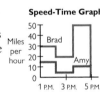

6. How far did each person travel?

### Extending Concepts

7. Find Thomas's speed during each time period. How did you figure it out? Make a speed-time graph to represent Thomas's trip.

8. If a speed-time graph stays flat, what does that tell you about the motion? What will the corresponding distance-time graph look like? If a speed-time graph slopes upward, what does that tell you about the motion? Why are there no sloping lines on your speed-time graph in item 7? Do you think this is realistic? Why or why not?

### Making Connections

9. An object dropped off a building accelerates because of gravity. Each second its speed increases by 32 feet per second—after 1 second its speed is 32 feet per second, after 2 seconds it is 64 feet per second, and so on. Which graph below could be a speed-time graph for an object dropped off a building? Which could be a distance-time graph? How you can tell?

a.

b.

c.

d.

# The Race Is On!

### Applying Skills

Below are the world's running records for men in different distances.

| Distance | Time |
|----------|------|
| 100 m | 9.8 sec |
| 400 m | 43.2 sec |
| 800 m | 1 min, 41 sec |
| 1,500 m | 3 min, 26 sec |

1. For each distance, find the average speed of the world champion runner.

2. How does the average speed change as the length of the race increases?

3. What would you predict for the world record for the men's 600-meter race? 1,200-meter race? 4,000-meter race?

4. Joel drove for 30 minutes at 40 miles per hour, for 1 hour at 60 miles per hour, and for 20 minutes at 54 miles per hour.

   a. How far did he travel at each speed?

   b. What was his total distance? his total time? his average speed?

   c. Create a total distance graph for Joel's trip.

### Extending Concepts

5. In a 20-mile bicycle race, Lois gave Sarah a head start of 15 minutes. Lois rode at an average speed of 22 miles per hour. Sarah rode at an average speed of 18 miles per hour. Who won the race? How did you find the answer? Make a total distance graph to show the race.

### Writing

6. Write a story to go with the speed-time graph shown here. Give speeds, distances, and directions for each person. Mark scales on the graph to match your story.

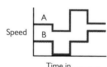

Draw a graph showing how the distance of each person from a certain point changes during the story. Tell where the distances are measured from. Find the average speed for each person.

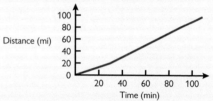

## Solutions: Lesson 11

1. 100 m: 10.2 m/sec; 400 m: 9.3 m/sec; 800 m: 7.9 m/sec; 1,500 m: 7.3 m/sec

2. It decreases.

3. Answers will vary.

4. a. 20 mi at 40 mph, 60 mi at 60 mph, 18 mi at 54 mph

   b. 98 mi; 1 hour, 50 min; 53.5 mph

   c.

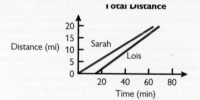

5. Sarah won.

6. Answers will vary.

## Solutions: Lesson 12

1. 12 mi; 6 hr      2. 2 mph
3. 1.33 mph; 2 mph; 3 mph   4. $d = 1.33t$; $d = 2t$; $d = 3t$
5.

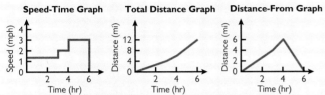

6–9. Answers will vary. Reports should include Jim: first 200 m: 6 m/sec; 33.3 sec; next 100 m: 9 m/sec; 11.1 sec; last 100 m: 10 m/sec; 10 sec; total time: 54.4 sec; average speed: 7.35 m/sec; Rajan: first 200 m: 9.1 m/sec; 22 sec; next 100 m: 5.6 m/sec; 18 sec; last 100 m: 4.5 m/sec; 22 sec; total time: 62 sec; average speed: 6.45 m/sec

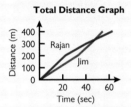 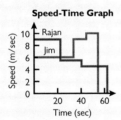

First 200 meters Rajan was faster, next 100 meters Jim was faster, last 100 meters Jim was faster. Jim passed Rajan after 48 sec; Jim won the race. Jim: first 200 m: $d = 6t$, $t = \frac{d}{6}$; next 100 m: $d = 9t$, $t = \frac{d}{9}$; last 100 m: $d = 10t$, $t = \frac{d}{10}$; Rajan: first 200 m: $d = 9.1t$, $t = \frac{d}{9.1}$; next 100 m: $d = 5.6t$, $t = \frac{d}{5.6}$; last 100 m: $d = 4.5t$, $t = \frac{d}{4.5}$

10.

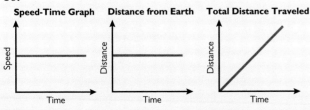

11. no; yes

# Final Project

### Applying Skills

Felix hiked up a mountain. During the first 3 hours, the trail was steep and he hiked only 4 miles. To hike the remaining 2 miles to the top took him 1 hour. It took him 2 hours to hike down again.

1. Find the total distance he walked and the total time.

2. Find his average speed for the whole trip.

3. Find his speed for each part of the trip.

4. For each part of the trip, find an equation that can be used to calculate distance traveled.

5. Make a speed-time graph, a graph showing the total distance traveled, and a graph showing distance from the starting point.

### Extending Concepts

Jim and Rajan ran a 400-meter race. Jim ran at 6 meters per second for the first 200 meters, 9 meters per second for the next 100, and at 10 meters per second for the last 100 meters. Rajan ran the first 200 meters in 22 seconds, the next 100 in 18 seconds, and the last 100 meters in 22 seconds. Use this data to write a report. Include the following:

6. For each person: the time and speed for each section of the race and the total time and average speed for the whole race.

7. Graphs showing total distance traveled and speed versus time.

8. Who was going faster during each period, at what times one person was passed by the other, and who won the race.

9. Equations that can be used to calculate time and/or distance for each person.

### Making Connections

Artificial satellites, which are placed in orbit around the earth, may be used for communications, research, meteorology, or navigation.

10. Suppose a satellite travels in a circular orbit about the earth at constant speed. Without showing any scale on the axes, sketch graphs showing total distance traveled, distance from the earth, and speed versus time while the satellite is in orbit.

11. Can you assume that an object is not moving if its distance-from graph is flat? if its total distance graph is flat? Explain your thinking.

# Assessment Overview

**M**any opportunities are offered in *Mathematics of Motion* to assess students' conceptual understanding and skills related to graphing and other representations of motion, making and using measurements and proportional reasoning, and algebraic equations. This unit contains embedded end-of-phase assessments in Lessons 4, 8, and 12, the last serving as the unit assessment. To start the unit, have students complete the pre-assessment activity on Teacher's Guide page 47E. Use this to assess readiness and growth throughout the unit. Also, you will find one skill quiz per phase on Reproducible pages R2–R4. Guidance for the optional use of portfolios is found on pages A18–A19.

The *MathScape* assessment system provides flexibility and support for educators. The core system uses three assessment tools to help you gather information, allowing you to monitor students' growth throughout the unit and evaluate knowledge at the unit end. Notes from the classroom share teachers' observations about student work, work evaluation, and ways to involve students in the assessment process.

# ASSESSMENT TOOLS

The three assessment tools—What To Look For, Assessment Rubric, and Skill Check—provide information for fully evaluating your students' learning. The information at the left shows where in the unit you can use each type of tool and on which Assessment page it is described.

## What To Look For

The What To Look For questions, which appear on the Teacher's Guide pages, are a short list of what students should be able to do at the end of an investigation. Use the questions as you lead a class discussion, monitor small group activities, or quickly check student work. The Assessment pages for these lessons provide an overview of student work along with teachers' observations.

## Assessment Rubric

The Assessment Rubric describes what student work might look like at each of four different levels. An Assessment Rubric is provided for each phase assessment and the unit assessment, where it is accompanied by student work and teachers' notes from the classroom. A reproducible of the Assessment Criteria, corresponding to level 3 of the Assessment Rubric, is also available for student use. A general assessment rubric is provided for evaluating portfolios, which are an optional part of the assessment system.

## Skill Check

The Skill Check helps you plan homework in the upcoming phase and review essential skills. It also provides the solutions for the Skill Quiz, a one-page reproducible quiz for each phase that focuses on the specific skills introduced or practiced in that phase. Teachers' notes contain suggestions on ways you can use the assessment information you gather to inform instruction.

## Reporting to Parents

Although not in itself an assessment tool, the Reporting to Parents page brings together the rich information gathered by the What To Look For, Assessment Rubric, and Skill Check tools, and provides guidance in assigning letter grades. If you need to assign one grade for the entire unit, the information gathered from the different assessment tools can be recorded on the Assessment Checklist, page A3, to help you maintain a balance between concepts, skills, and processes.

# ASSESSMENT CHECKLIST

**T**he Assessment Checklist is on Reproducible page R1. You can use it to record the information gathered about each student with the different assessment tools and to note your observations. You can also give students their own copies of the checklist, which they can use to organize and reflect on their work for their portfolios.

The assessment checklist is a handy one-sheet tool that allows me to keep the overall picture in mind when planning activities and helps me, when I'm planning, to see if other skill activities or homework lessons need to be assigned or taught. I also use the assessment checklist when talking to my principal about objectives for the year. It helps keep my principal apprised of what instruction is going on in the classroom. □

The Notes column is a great place for students to write down hints about what they may need to remember when they get home. I also encourage them to write down their scores after they have corrected their homework. I give students a chance to revise any homework prior to the end of a phase. □

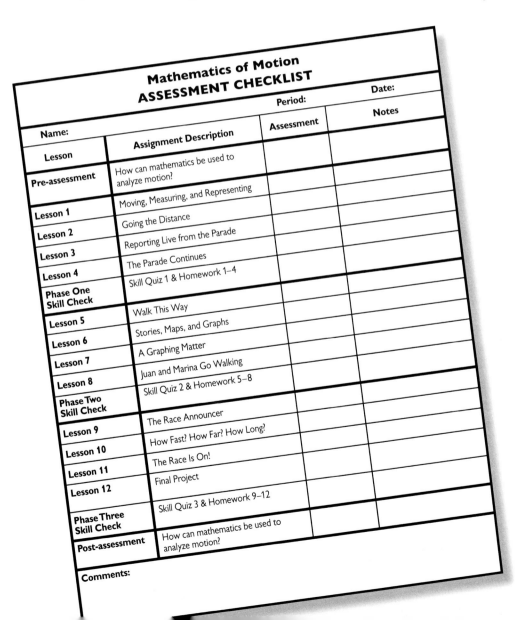

### Mathematics of Motion
### ASSESSMENT CHECKLIST

Period: _____  Date: _____

| Name: | Assignment Description | Assessment | Notes |
|---|---|---|---|
| **Lesson** | | | |
| Pre-assessment | How can mathematics be used to analyze motion? | | |
| Lesson 1 | Moving, Measuring, and Representing | | |
| Lesson 2 | Going the Distance | | |
| Lesson 3 | Reporting Live from the Parade | | |
| Lesson 4 | The Parade Continues | | |
| Phase One Skill Check | Skill Quiz 1 & Homework 1–4 | | |
| Lesson 5 | Walk This Way | | |
| Lesson 6 | Stories, Maps, and Graphs | | |
| Lesson 7 | A Graphing Matter | | |
| Lesson 8 | Juan and Marina Go Walking | | |
| Phase Two Skill Check | Skill Quiz 2 & Homework 5–8 | | |
| Lesson 9 | The Race Announcer | | |
| Lesson 10 | How Fast? How Far? How Long? | | |
| Lesson 11 | The Race Is On! | | |
| Lesson 12 | Final Project | | |
| Phase Three Skill Check | Skill Quiz 3 & Homework 9–12 | | |
| Post-assessment | How can mathematics be used to analyze motion? | | |

Comments:

# Assessment

*About half my class had trouble using metric units and converting them to U.S. units, and with making measurements and computing averages. We held a mini-workshop with practice problems in these topics to bolster confidence and skills before beginning the unit.* □

**WHAT TO LOOK FOR**

# Pre-assessment

**Y**ou can use the Pre-assessment on page 47E of the Teacher's Guide to assess the prerequisites for the unit. At the end of the unit, you can compare this task to Lesson 11 to note growth that has occurred in the course of the unit. (See Post-assessment, page A17.)

**DO STUDENTS' PRE-ASSESSMENTS DEMONSTRATE THE PREREQUISITES OF:**

- an ability to accurately measure time and distance?

- knowledge of U.S. standard and metric units, including inches, feet, yards, miles, centimeters, meters, kilometers?

- understanding of the idea of an average?

Steps 1-3

| Objects that move | Units of Measurment |
|---|---|
| 1. car | 1. mph |
| 2. feet | 2. steps per min. |
| 3. boat | 3. mph |
| 4. hands | 4. waves per min. |
| 5. cat | 5. feet per sec. |
| 6. blender | 6. RPM |
| 7. microwave tray | 7. rpm |
| 8. vibrating chair | 8. cycles per second |
| 9. eylids | 9. blinkes per min. |
| 10. wind | 10. mph |
| 11. basketball | 11. mph |
| 12. falling rain | 12. mph |
| 13. egg beater | 13. rpm |
| 14. second hand of clock | 14. rpm |
| 15. fan | 15. rpm |
| 16. egg slicer | 16. slices per min. |
| 17. bicycle wheel | 17. rpm |
| 18. conveyer belt | 18. feet per min. |
| 19. person | 19. mph |
| 20. soap sliding | 20. inches per sec |
| 21. air plane | 21. mph |
| 22. garbage disposal | 22. rpm |

per: means for each

* They all have the word per
* They all have 3 words
* They all end with time
* They all begin with movement

# Phase One: Lessons 1, 2 & 3

The student work from Lessons 1, 2, and 3 of this phase should show an increased understanding of the mathematical relationships among distance, time, and speed. One common error to look for in students' work is that they may determine speed by time alone rather than by distance per unit of time. Some students may believe that a motion that takes a short time must be fast and a motion that occurs over a long time must be slow.

*As I was walking around the room listening to small-group discussions, I realized that almost half of my students were not visualizing the parade going down a straight street, but instead were seeing characters moving in a diagonal path—they mentally connected the adjacent snapshots. By making a transparency of the characters in place on the Snapshot Sequence Sheet and cutting it in strips, the students were able to see how the characters moved in a straight path over time. ☐*

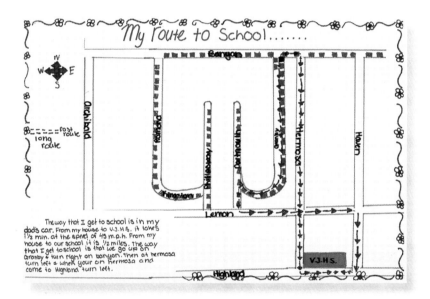

*I had several papers at level 4. Some of my students did show a deep understanding of the relationship between distance, time, and speed, and created realistic and interesting stories. These students not only applied what was taught but took the next step to create something new.* □

*One paper showed a clear connection between time, distance, and speed, with only a few errors. The story imitated the simple format of the previous lessons and read like a word or story problem, but had no real connection to the real world. I encouraged the student to revise the story to include more details. I gave this work a 3.*

*One of my students didn't notice that the landmarks were not evenly spaced as in previous lessons. When I pointed this out, the student was unable to apply what the student had learned to this new situation. When I modified the lesson to make the spacing even, the student was able to do the operation, but was still unable to explain the relationship between time and distance. I gave this work a 2.* □

# Phase One: Lesson 4

**F**or the embedded assessment in **Lesson 4, The Parade Continues,** students applied what they had learned in Phase One to write snapshot stories—narratives that interpret visual representations of motion. The Assessment Rubric on the opposite page is designed to help you evaluate student work. See Reproducible page **R5** for a version of the level 3 assessment criteria worded for student use.

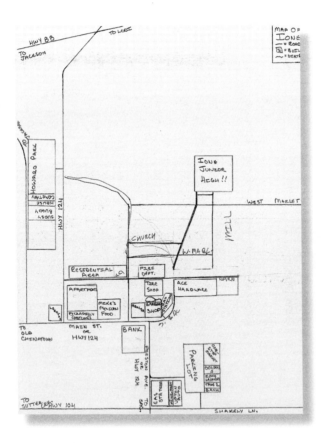

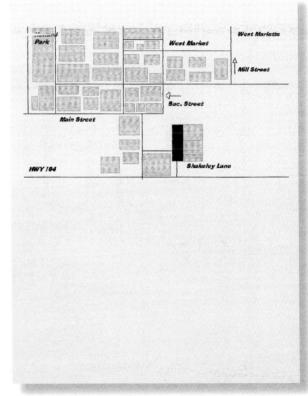

# *Does student work ...*

- make sound estimates of distance, time, and speed?

- show consistent ability to determine distance, time, or speed when two of these are known?

- include detailed and creative visual and verbal representations of motion, including a trip to school?

- show development of a correct equation for distance traveled as a function of speed and time?

- demonstrate a deep understanding of how linear motion, stationary position, distance traveled, time, speed, direction, change in speed, and relative motion are represented in a snapshot sequence?

- interpolate values accurately in a snapshot sequence?

 **Goes beyond expectations**

- make reasonable estimates of distance, time, and speed?

- show ability to estimate distance, time, or speed when two of these variables are given?

- include fairly detailed visual and verbal representations of various kinds of motion, including a trip to school?

- show development of a correct written equation for distance traveled as a function of speed and time?

- demonstrate an understanding of how stationary position, distance traveled, time, speed, direction, and relative motion are represented in a snapshot sequence?

- interpolate values in a snapshot sequence with few errors?

 **Meets all expectations**

- feature unrealistic initial estimates and no improvement in ability to estimate distance, time, and speed?

- show unreasonable estimates of distance, time, or speed when given two of these variables?

- include visual and verbal representations of various kinds of motion that do not contain basic characteristics of motion such as speed, distance traveled, and time spent, or that contain many errors?

- provide an incorrect equation or written expression for distance traveled as a function of speed and time?

- interpolate values in a snapshot sequence inconsistently?

 **Meets some expectations**

- make unreasonable estimates of distance, time, and speed?

- show inability to determine distance, time, or speed when two of these variables are known?

- include inaccurate or incomplete visual and verbal representations of various kinds of motion, including a trip to school?

- provide no equation or expression for distance traveled as a function of speed and time?

- demonstrate little or no evidence of understanding how distance traveled, time, speed, direction, change in speed, or relative motion are represented in a snapshot sequence?

- show inability to interpolate values in a snapshot sequence?

 **Falls below expectations**

# Assessment

*I found that some of my students needed help calculating distance, time, or speed. Although they were familiar with the operations, they had not made the connection to the real world. As a class, we worked through calculating how long it would take us to get to various parts of the school based on how long it took us to walk 10 feet. I supplemented this with the skill practice in the homework. □*

## SKILL CHECK

# Phase One: Homework & Quiz

**S**tudents' conceptual understanding in Phase One is monitored daily using **What To Look For** and evaluated using the **Assessment Rubric**. The lesson homework and the **Phase One Skill Quiz** are tools to check skill proficiency.

## Homework

Homework for Lessons 1–4 appears in the Student Guide on pages 78–81. Depending on the needs of your students, you may assign all or part of the homework for each lesson. You may want to take students' homework performance into consideration as part of the overall phase evaluation.

## Skill Quiz

The Phase One Skill Quiz is provided on Reproducible page R2. Solutions are given here. Hot Topics for Phase One are:

- Systems of Measurement

- Length and Distance

- Setting Up Expressions and Equations

- Displaying Data

### SKILL QUIZ ANSWERS

1. **a.** 4 mph, 2 m/sec     **b.** 600 ft/sec
   **c.** 20 m/sec, 50 mph     **d.** 8 mph, 12 ft/sec

2. 4 ft; 240 ft; 14,400 ft; 1,320 sec or 22 min

3. 84 mi; 17 ft/sec; 15 min

4. **a.** 5 mph     **b.** 20 mph

5. 72 m

6. 6 sec

7. A: 12 m, B: 0 m, C: 18 m;
   A: 2 m/sec, B: 0 m/sec, C: 3 m/sec; C

8. 3rd snapshot: A: at Booth 3, B: at Booth 7, C: at Booth 4
   4th snapshot: A: at Booth 4, B: at Booth 7, C: 6 m past Booth 5

9. A: 600 m, B: 0 m, C: 900 m; A: 960 m, B: 0 m, C: 1,440 m

10. Answers will vary.

# Phase Two: Lessons 5, 6 & 7

The student work from Lessons 5, 6, and 7 of this phase should show an increased understanding of how visual representations, especially distance-time graphs, can describe motion. One common error to look for in students' work is overly concrete interpretation of graphs. They may confuse graphs with pictorial representations, believing for example that slope represents the angle of incline of an object moving uphill.

*Lesson 5 provided one of those "aha" moments for many of my students. As they worked with the simultaneous journeys of Pedro and Tanya, it became obvious which students were interpreting the graphs to create a real-life context, and which students were just manipulating numbers. One student who was able to connect the graph of Pedro and Tanya's journey to a real-life situation summed it up when she looked at the graph and said, "Hey, where was Pedro before 8:15?"* ☐

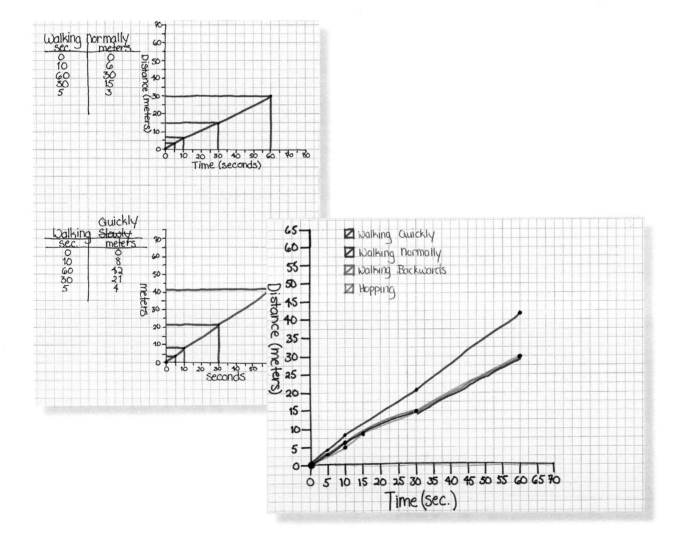

*One of my students went far beyond my expectations by plotting curves on a graph and exploring negative and positive slope. The student's creative story showed growth from the previous phase and maintained the details as it converted among stories, maps, and graphs. I gave this paper a 4.* □

*In this phase, I was pleased to see many creative stories that had detailed and realistic settings. One student grasped the concept that two things can happen at the same time and was able to show the relationship between the time, distance, and speed of each activity. The student's analysis of the graphs was perfect, but the original graphs had a few mistakes and were simplistic. I gave this paper a 3.* □

*I gave the paper a 2 if the student was able to accurately analyze the graphs but had real difficulty creating an original graph. I pointed out that although you can move backward in distance, you cannot move back in time. Some students also had problems describing the relationship between time, distance, and speed.* □

**I**n Lesson 8, Juan and Marina Go Walking, students applied what they had learned in Phase Two to compare graphs and stories describing changes over time. The Assessment Rubric on the opposite page is designed to help you evaluate student work. See Reproducible page R5 for a version of the level 3 assessment criteria worded for student use.

### 2  Going the Distance

**Estimating, Measuring, and Calculating Distance**

To find out how far it is from one point to another, do you estimate the distance? Measure it? Calculate it? In this lesson, you will have the chance to use all three ways of determining distance.

#### Finding Out How Far

*When you move from here to there, how do you know how far you have gone?*

1. Without actually walking or measuring, *estimate* how far you will go in 10 seconds when moving in each way shown in the table below. Record your estimates in the table.

2. After you record your estimates, work with your partners to measure how far you *actually* go in 10 seconds for each way of moving.

| | Estimate: Distance in 10 seconds | Measure: Distance in 10 seconds | Calculate: Distance in 1 second | Calc Dist 1 mi |
|---|---|---|---|---|
| | meters | meters | meters | m |
| Walking at your regular pace | 10 | 10 | 1 | 6 |
| Walking quickly | 17 | 14 | 1.4 | 8 |
| Hopping | 9 | 13 | 1.3 | 7 |
| Walking backwards | 10 | 14 | 1.4 | 8 |
| A way of moving you make up | | | | |

*How do your estimates compare with ... you surprised by any of the results?*

quick pace
14 \ 12.5
14 \ 12.11
22.32 \ 13.09
17.6 \ 14
20.34 \ 14
14.69 \ 14.69
20.93 \ 17.6 } 17.6
30 \ 20.34
23.95 \ 20.93
24.25 \ 22.32
12.5 \ 23.95
12.11 \ 24.25
13.09 \ 30

hopping pace
5.75
9.5
10.8
11.73
12.5
13
13 } 13.6
14.27
14.92
15.8
23.45
23.9
25.02
30

Backwards pace
14 \ 7.33
14 \ 10.05
14 \ 10.67
11 \ 11
19.24 \ 11
10.67 \ 11
16.96 \ 14 } 14
20 \ 14
10.05 \ 14
20.57 \ 15.3
15.3 \ 16.96
14 \ 19.24
14 \ 20
7.33 \ 20.57

I calculated column three by dividing column two by ten.

I calculated column four by multiplying column three by 60.

I calculated column five by multiplying column four by 60.

I calculated column six by taking ... ding it by column four.

Average
1.65 \ 12.5
13.18 \ 17.4
4.31 \ 16.0
2.11 \ 13.9

20÷2=10.125≈10.1

# *Does student work ...*

- show correct labeling and scaling of axes and plotting of curves on various kinds of graphs?

- make accurate interpretations of positive slope, negative slope, constant slope, and zero slope on distance-time graphs?

- demonstrate an ability to convert among stories, maps, and graphs?

- identify physically impossible distance-time graphs?

- create, compare, and convert among distance-from, distance-to, and total distance graphs?

- design walking routes that can be described by the three types of distance-time graphs explored in Phase Two?

**Goes beyond expectations**

- show correct labeling and scaling of axes on various kinds of graphs?

- make accurate interpretations of slope as speed on distance-time graphs?

- demonstrate an ability to retain most of the mathematically important information while converting among stories, maps, and graphs?

- identify physically impossible distance-time graphs ?

- create and compare distance-from, distance-to, and total distance graphs?

- design walking routes that can be described by the three types of distance-time graphs explored in Phase Two?

**Meets all expectations**

- show some correct labeling and scaling of axes on various kinds of graphs?

- demonstrate some understanding that slope represents speed on distance-time graphs?

- show an ability to retain some of the mathematically important information while converting among stories, maps, and graphs?

- identify some physically impossible distance-time graphs?

- distinguish how distance-from, distance-to, and total distance graphs differ from one another?

- design walking routes that can be described by the three types of distance-time graphs explored in Phase Two?

**Meets some expectations**

- show usually incorrect labeling and scaling of axes on various kinds of graphs?

- demonstrate no understanding that slope represents speed on distance-time graphs?

- show inability to retain information when converting among stories, maps, and graphs?

- show inability to recognize impossible distance-time graphs?

- show inability to describe the distinguishing features of distance-from, distance-to, and total distance graphs?

- design a walking route that cannot be described by distance-time graphs explored in Phase Two?

**Falls below expectations**

SKILL CHECK

# Phase Two: Homework & Quiz

**S**tudents' conceptual understanding in **Phase Two** is monitored daily using **What To Look For** and evaluated using the **Assessment Rubric**. The lesson homework and the **Phase Two Skill Quiz** are ways to check skill proficiency.

## Homework

Homework for Lessons 5–8 appears in the Student Guide on pages 82–85.

## Skill Quiz

The Phase Two Skill Quiz is provided on Reproducible page R3. Solutions are given here. Hot Topics for Phase Two are:

- Graphing on the Coordinate Plane
- Displaying Data
- Slope and Intercept

### SKILL QUIZ ANSWERS

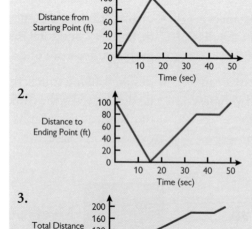

**4.** a, c, d    **5.** c; d    **6.** 4; map

**7.** Between 3:50 P.M. and 4:00 P.M.; between 3:40 P.M. and 3:50 P.M. he was not moving away from school at all; graph

**8.** 10 min; graph    **9.** south; map

**10.** To get his homework; story

**11. a.** Not consistent; Connor's graph shows he stopped for 10 minutes to look for his homework; Dan stopped for only 5 minutes.

**b.** Answers will vary.

# Phase Three: Lessons 9, 10 & 11

The student work from Lessons 9, 10, and 11 of this phase should show an increased understanding of distance-time graphs showing variable speeds and growing familiarity with the distinction between average speed and instantaneous speed and the graphical representation of each. One common error to look for in students' work is the attempt to find average speed by checking the slope of a distance-time graph at a particular point.

*My students loved Lesson 9. I had them announce the various sporting events in front of the classroom, and then allowed the audience to ask questions. The dialogue was helpful to those students who were still unsure of the relationship between time, distance, and speed. Many students asked if they could rewrite the assignment in light of the presentations and questions. □*

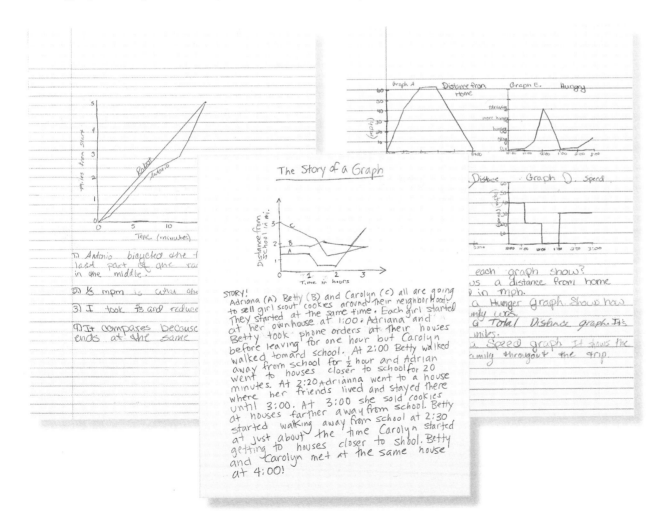

# Phase Three: Lesson 12

*Because the rubric covered all the major skills of Phase Three, I felt that it was a fair and appropriate assessment tool. It also produced a class curve that was in line with what I would have predicted. About 20% of my students earned 4s, about 40% got 3s, 20% received 2s, and only 10% got 1s.*

*I added another factor to my evaluation criteria besides those that are listed in the rubric. The additional factor was effort; I wanted to reward my students for trying hard even if their content mastery lagged behind. □*

**I**n Lesson 12, students applied what they had learned in the unit to the Final Project. They had to choose a particular example of motion to study, then collect, analyze, and present data and information describing that motion. The Assessment Rubric on the opposite page is designed to help you evaluate student work. See Reproducible page R5 for a version of the level 3 assessment criteria worded for student use.

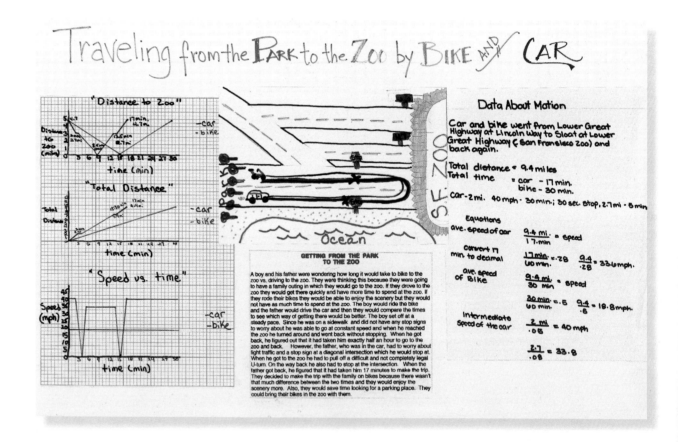

# Does student work ...

- thoroughly and correctly describe the running, swimming, and three-legged races?

- graph all of the important information found in race commentaries?

- show deep understanding of average speed and ability to obtain it from a graph?

- exhibit ability to construct an error-free distance-time graph and speed-time graph?

- show excellent ability to use algebraic equations to solve for distance, speed, and time?

- demonstrate mastery of graphing skills, including labeling and scaling axes, converting between graphs and stories, and using graphs to check solutions?

 **Goes beyond expectations**

- correctly describe the running, swimming, and three-legged races?

- graph with few errors most of the information in commentaries on the running, swimming, and three-legged races?

- show good understanding of the concept of average speed?

- exhibit ability to construct a generally correct distance-time graph and speed-time graph?

- use algebraic equations consistently to solve for distance, speed, and time?

- show satisfactory achievement of graphing skills, including labeling and scaling axes, converting between graphs and stories, and using graphs to check solutions?

 **Meets all expectations**

- describe running, swimming, and three-legged races mostly correctly?

- include graphs that contain some errors but also some information found in race commentaries?

- show elementary understanding of average speed?

- exhibit ability to construct a partly correct distance-time graph and speed-time graph?

- demonstrate ability to state algebraic equations to solve for distance, speed, and time?

- show intermittent success with various graphing skills, including labeling and scaling axes, converting between graphs and stories, and using graphs to check algebraic solutions?

 **Meets some expectations**

- include largely incorrect and very undetailed descriptions of the motions in running, swimming, and three-legged races?

- graph almost none of the information in race commentaries?

- show no understanding of the concept of average speed?

- exhibit inability to construct a correct distance-time graph and speed-time graph?

- demonstrate inability to state algebraic equations to solve for distance, speed, and time?

- show little facility with graphing skills, including labeling and scaling axes, converting between graphs and stories, and using graphs to check solutions?

 **Falls below expectations**

# Assessment

**SKILL CHECK**

# Phase Three: Homework & Quiz

**S**tudents' conceptual understanding in **Phase Three** is monitored daily using the **What To Look For** and evaluated using the **Assessment Rubric.**

## Homework

Homework for Lessons 9–12 appears in the Student Guide on pages 86–89.

## Skill Quiz

The Phase Three Skill Quiz is on Reproducible page R4. Solutions are given here. Hot Topics for Phase Three are: ▪ Graphing on the Coordinate Plane; ▪ Evaluating Expressions and Formulas; ▪ Slope and Intercept

### SKILL QUIZ ANSWERS

1. 10 sec and 15 sec
2. At around 22 sec
3. Tony: 35 sec; Bruce: 30 sec; Bruce
4. 200 m; Bruce: 6.7 m/sec; Tony: 5.7 m/sec
5. 6.7 m/sec

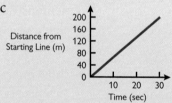

6. 8 m/sec; 0 m/sec; 6 m/sec

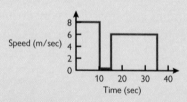

7. Answers will vary.
8. On a speed-time graph, the height of the graph shows speed. On a total distance graph, a steeper graph shows faster motion.

9. C; it reflects speeds of 0.5 mps, 1 mps, 0.5 mps, and 2 mps.
10. a. 7 mi; 10 mi; 9 mi

    b. 40 min at 12 mph; 80 min at 9 mph; 1 hr at 6 mph

    c. Nancy: 26 mi; 4 hr; 6.5 mph; Lisa: 26 mi; 3 hr; 8.7 mph; Lisa

    d.

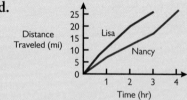

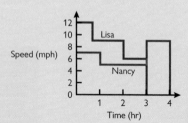

11. 50 mph

# Post-assessment

To get a sense of your students' growth over the course of the unit, you can compare students' pre-assessment work (see page A4) with their final project. Ask students to write a second response to the question: **How can mathematics be used to analyze motion? Compare this to their pre-assessment writing.**

*I had students use the rubric in the student book to grade their own work. I also gave each a copy of the rubric I used, which showed how I computed their grade. Students then wrote a paragraph describing whether our two rubrics agreed closely and whether they felt my assessment reflected the true value of their work. In cases where students did not agree with my assessment, I gave them the opportunity to meet with me to use their rubrics to argue their case. In a few cases, I adjusted students' grades based on what they said. □*

## DID STUDENTS DEMONSTRATE GROWTH IN:

- ability to use distance-from, distance-to, and total distance graphs?

- constructing graphs that represent change over time, including graphs of distance versus time and speed versus time?

- interpreting features of graphs, including slope (e.g., changes in slope, constant slope, zero slope, and negative slope)?

- converting among stories, graphs, and maps that represent motion?

- using algebraic equations to solve for speed, distance, and time in motion problems?

# Assessment

*Portfolios can be comprised only of student-selected work. Given a few criteria, like "Choose five of your best pieces of work," students can make their own choices regarding what to put into the portfolio. This leaves the specific choice of work up to them entirely; however, I need to be sure that they show a range of activities or lessons. To make sure that they have included different types of activities or lessons, I specify different areas to choose from: one from applying skills, one from extending concepts, and so on. Also, I ask them to include a paragraph or two regarding why they made these choices and what the selections show in terms of math. This method works especially well if you are using any type of standards-based assessment. For example, I shared two or three of the standards and asked students to choose work that showed how they met or exceeded the standard. □*

**4 3 2 1 ASSESSMENT RUBRIC**

# Portfolio Review

The focus of the portfolio evaluation is to gain insight into students' growth over time and to see how they view themselves as mathematicians. The portfolio should show students' increasing ability to communicate mathematically, solve problems, and make mathematical connections. The Assessment Rubric on the opposite page is designed to help you evaluate student work.

**FOR THIS UNIT THE FOLLOWING ITEMS WORK ESPECIALLY WELL TO SUPPLEMENT A STUDENT'S BASIC PORTFOLIO:**

- a problem made up by the student, with a solution

- writing about mathematics in the student's primary language

- an autobiography describing the student's mathematical growth over time

- a report of a group project, with a description of how the student contributed

- student work from another subject area using mathematics

# *Does the portfolio show ...*

- significant mathematical growth in the understanding and application of unit goals?

- significant mathematical growth in skill development?

- creativity and quality of work that goes beyond the assignment?

- timely completion of assignments?

- no significant mathematical errors in assigned work?

- clear, coherent, and thoughtful explanations of the mathematical process?

**Goes beyond expectations**

- some mathematical growth in the understanding and application of unit goals?

- some mathematical growth in skill development?

- acceptable quality of work?

- timely completion of assignments?

- no significant mathematical errors in assigned work?

- clear explanations of the mathematical process?

**Meets all expectations**

- an understanding and application of unit goals?

- skill development documented with little growth?

- inconsistent quality of work?

- assignments that are complete but not always on time?

- minor mathematical errors in the assigned work?

- unclear explanations of the mathematical process?

**Meets some expectations**

- that key points in the understanding and application of unit goals were missed?

- that skill development is not documented?

- consistently poor quality of work?

- that assignments are consistently late?

- significant mathematical errors in assigned work?

- no explanations of the mathematical process?

**Falls below expectations**

# Assessment

*I used the phase assessments in a number of ways. Sometimes I graded them as tests; however, I also graded some phase assessments with the same weight as a lesson grade. Usually lessons count 2 or 3 times as much as homework counts. The phase assessment grade depends on how long it took the class to finish the assignment: if it took 2 days, then it is worth 2 homework grades; if it took 3 days, then it's worth 3 grades. The final project is always worth more than the first two assessments.* □

*Self-assessments by my students are used in portfolios, group work, presentations, projects, and so on. Using a rubric, they determine what score they deserve in terms of learning and performing, but they need to justify or explain why. They can assess the group work in terms of effort, quality, and performance. Students also take part in forming the assessment criteria, up front, before the project or group work begins, so that there is no confusion on their part about expectations.* □

# Reporting to Parents

**If you need to assign a single letter grade to reflect all the rich information students have gathered over the course of the unit, remember to maintain a balance between concepts, skills, and processes when doing so. In this particular unit, the final project is cumulative, and the rubric score from the project should be a large part of any grade given.**

## Skill Proficiency

By combining the Skill Checks, homework, and any Handbook assignments, you should be able to demonstrate to parents their child's ability to practice the skills involving graphing motion beyond the contexts of the in-class investigations. Although graphing skills are an integral part of the daily lessons in this unit, an obvious example to show parents how skills are incorporated into an investigation is Lesson 7, A Graphing Matter, in which students make three types of distance-time graphs.

## Conceptual Understanding

In this unit, the concepts covered in the embedded phase assessments for Phases One and Two are also incorporated into the final project at the end of Phase Three. As a result, parents can see their child's conceptual understanding of characteristics of motion from Phase One, combined with the work with narratives and graphs in Phase Two, demonstrated in the final project they produce in Lesson 12, Final Project. You can also use Lesson 8, Juan and Marina Go Walking, as a

specific example to demonstrate to parents how an investigation introduces various kinds of graphs that are an essential foundation for the study of graphing in high school.

## Mathematical Processes

Problem solving and mathematical communication occur regularly in daily lessons. The final project is ideal for showing parents the nature of the problem-solving and mathematical communication processes in which their child is engaged. The problem situation of analyzing motion and communicating about the motion involved in a subject of their own interest in writing and oral presentation are rich, real-world experiences for the student. You may want to invite parents to visit the class for a "Seminar on Motion" to see the students' completed final projects.

# Mathematics of Motion
# ASSESSMENT CHECKLIST

**Name:**                       **Period:**         **Date:**

| Lesson | Assignment Description | Assessment | Notes |
|---|---|---|---|
| **Pre-assessment** | How can mathematics be used to analyze motion? | | |
| **Lesson 1** | Moving, Measuring, and Representing | | |
| **Lesson 2** | Going the Distance | | |
| **Lesson 3** | Reporting Live from the Parade | | |
| **Lesson 4** | The Parade Continues | | |
| **Phase One Skill Check** | Skill Quiz 1 & Homework 1–4 | | |
| **Lesson 5** | Walk This Way | | |
| **Lesson 6** | Stories, Maps, and Graphs | | |
| **Lesson 7** | A Graphing Matter | | |
| **Lesson 8** | Juan and Marina Go Walking | | |
| **Phase Two Skill Check** | Skill Quiz 2 & Homework 5–8 | | |
| **Lesson 9** | The Race Announcer | | |
| **Lesson 10** | How Fast? How Far? How Long? | | |
| **Lesson 11** | The Race Is On! | | |
| **Lesson 12** | Final Project | | |
| **Phase Three Skill Check** | Skill Quiz 3 & Homework 9–12 | | |
| **Post-assessment** | How can mathematics be used to analyze motion? | | |

**Comments:**

PHASE ONE
# Skill Quiz

1. For each motion, tell which of these speeds are possible: 20 meters per second, 8 miles per hour, 4 miles per hour, 12 feet per second, 2 meters per second, 50 miles per hour, 600 feet per second, 25 feet per hour.

   **a.** a person walking          **b.** a plane flying

   **c.** a gazelle running at full speed          **d.** a person jogging

2. Suppose that you walk backward 80 feet in 20 seconds. At that rate, how far would you walk in 1 second? in 1 minute? in 1 hour? How long would it take to go 1 mile?

3. Copy and complete the table below. Include the appropriate units.

| Distance | Time | Speed |
|---|---|---|
|  | 2.8 hours | 30 miles per hour |
| 561 feet | 33 seconds |  |
| 180 meters |  | 12 meters per minute |

4. Julie runs the length of her backyard at a speed of 10 miles per hour.

   **a.** If José runs the length of the yard and takes twice as long, how fast was he going?

   **b.** If Dan runs four times the length of the yard and takes twice as long as Julie, how fast was he going?

The field notes below give the positions of unknown characters A, B, and C in a parade. The parade is moving along a street from Booth 1 towards Booth 8. The distance between booths is 12 meters.

1st Snapshot, 3:50:00 P.M.

  A: At Booth 1

  B: At Booth 7

  C: At Booth 1

2nd Snapshot, 3:50:06 P.M.

  A: At Booth 2

  B: At Booth 7

  C: 6 meters past Booth 2

3rd and 4th snapshots

  Too cloudy

5th Snapshot, 3:50:24 P.M.

  A: At Booth 5

  B: At Booth 7

  C: At Booth 7

5. How far is it from Booth 1 to Booth 7?

6. How much time is there between consecutive snapshots?

7. How far does each character travel between snapshots? What is the speed of each character? Who is traveling the fastest?

8. Find the position of each character for the 3rd and 4th snapshots.

9. How far would each character travel in 5 minutes? in 8 minutes?

10. Write a story explaining this snapshot sequence. Explain who the characters are and what is at each booth. Give the speeds of the characters and explain why they are moving at that speed.

## PHASE TWO
# Skill Quiz

To reach the end of the hallway, Kevin walked 100 feet in a straight line in 15 seconds. He walked back 80 feet toward the starting point in 20 seconds, waited 10 seconds, then walked all the way back to the starting point in 5 seconds.

**1.** Make a graph showing his distance from the starting point versus time.

**2.** Make a graph showing his distance to the ending point versus time.

**3.** Make a graph showing the total distance Kevin walked versus time.

**4.** Which graph(s) below could represent distance from a point?

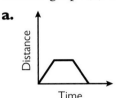 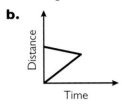  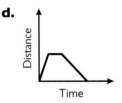

**5.** Which graph in item **4** could be a total distance graph? Identify a second graph that could be a distance-from graph for the same motion.

Use the story, map, and graph to answer the questions. Tell whether you used the story, the map, or the graph to find each answer.

Connor left school at 3:30 P.M. to walk home. He went a little way and then realized he had forgotten his homework. He walked back to school, searched everywhere for his homework, finally found it, and left school again, this time in a hurry. He ran all the way home.

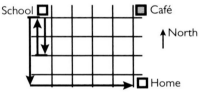

**6.** How many streets does Connor cross between his home and the café?

**7.** When was Connor traveling away from school the fastest? the slowest?

**8.** How long did Connor spend searching for his homework?

**9.** In what direction was Connor traveling when he first left school?

**10.** Why did Connor go back again to school?

**11.a.** Tell whether the story below is consistent with Connor's distance-from graph above and the total distance graph shown here. Explain how you can tell.

"Dan and Connor left school together at 3:30 P.M. After a little while they both turned around and went back to school again. Dan waited while Connor looked for his homework, and then they walked home together."

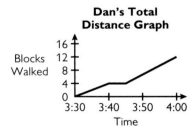

**b.** Write your own story that is consistent with Connor's distance-from graph above and Dan's total distance graph. Make a third graph showing how one of the characters felt during the story.

PHASE THREE
# Skill Quiz

Use the graph of the running race for items **1–7**.

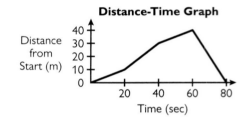

**1.** At what times were there changes in speed?

**2.** At what time did Bruce pass Tony?

**3.** How long did each person take to complete the race? Who won?

**4.** How far did each person run? What was the average speed for each person?

**5.** If you program a robot to roll at a constant speed in the race, at what speed should it roll to tie Bruce? Draw a graph of the robot's race.

**6.** What is Tony's speed at 5 seconds? at 12 seconds? 30 seconds? Make a speed-time graph to represent Tony's race.

**7.** Write a commentary for the running race. Describe what is happening as fully and as accurately as you can.

**8.** Suppose you have a speed-time graph and a total distance graph, each showing the motion of two people during a race. Explain how you can use each graph to tell who is moving fastest during a certain period.

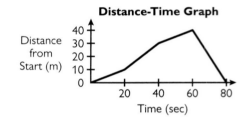

**9.** The distance-time graph at right shows a 2-lap swimming race. Which speed-time graph below could represent the same race? How can you tell?

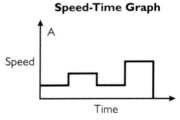

**Speed-Time Graph**

A

Speed

Time

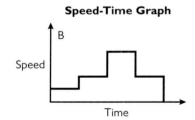

**Speed-Time Graph**

B

Speed

Time

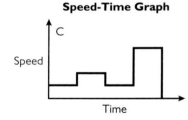

**Speed-Time Graph**

C

Speed

Time

**10.** Nancy and Lisa ran a marathon race. Nancy ran for 1 hour at 7 miles per hour, for 2 hours at 5 miles per hour, and for 1 hour at 9 miles per hour. Lisa ran 8 miles at 12 miles per hour, 12 miles at 9 miles per hour, and 6 miles at 6 miles per hour.

**a.** How far did Nancy run at each speed?

**b.** For what length of time did Lisa travel at each speed?

**c.** For each person find the total distance, the total time, and the average speed. Who won the race?

**d.** Make graphs showing total distance traveled and speed versus time for the race.

**11.** Ralph drove to work. He drove for 20 minutes at 30 miles per hour and for 40 minutes at 60 miles per hour. What was his average speed?

# Student Assessment Criteria

PHASE ONE
## Does my work show that I can ...

- make reasonable estimates of distance, time, and speed?

- estimate distance, time, or speed when I know two of these quantities?

- provide detailed visual and written representations of different kinds of motion, including a trip to school?

- write an expression that shows how distance can be determined from speed and time?

- understand how a snapshot sequence shows position, distance, time, speed, direction, and the motion of one parade character compared to another?

- find missing data in a snapshot sequence?

PHASE TWO
## Does my work show that I can ...

- label and scale the axes of different kinds of graphs?

- interpret what the slope of a distance-time graph means?

- convert among stories, maps, and graphs, keeping the important mathematical information intact?

- identify impossible distance-time graphs?

- create distance-from, distance-to, and total distance graphs?

- compare distance-from, distance-to, and total distance graphs?

- design walking routes that can be described by the three types of distance-time graphs?

PHASE THREE
## Does my work show that I can ...

- write commentaries that describe graphs of running, swimming, and three-legged races?

- make graphs from race commentaries?

- understand average speed and obtain average speed from a distance-time graph?

- construct a distance-time graph and a speed-time graph?

- use equations to solve for distance, speed, and time?

- use various graphing skills, including labeling and scaling axes, converting between graphs and stories, and using graphs to check algebraic solutions?

Dear Family,

Our class will soon be investigating motion by studying a unit called *Mathematics of Motion: Distance, Speed, and Time.* In this unit, students will use measurement, algebra, and graphing skills to describe motion verbally, visually, graphically, and mathematically.

Students will begin by measuring speed, distance, and time of familiar motions and motions of their own choosing. They will then learn how to use a Snapshot Sequence Sheet, a series of schematic pictures of a parade taken from a bird's-eye view. The Snapshot Sequence Sheet is a concrete representation of motion that sets the stage for introducing distance-time graphs in a subsequent lesson.

When students begin making and analyzing graphs, they learn that there are three kinds of useful distance-time graphs: the *distance-from* graph, that represents distance traveled from a given point as a function of time; the *distance-to* graph, that shows how far an object has to travel to reach a given point at any given time; and the *total distance* graph, that shows the cumulative distance moved by an object in any direction over time.

*Mathematics of Motion* gives students the tools to create and analyze graphs by teaching them the meaning of slope and how to scale and label axes and plot points.

In the unit, students practice comparing various representations of motion: maps, written descriptions, graphs, and other forms. They learn what the benefits and limitations are of each kind of representation.

Problem solving is another major thrust of *Mathematics of Motion.* Students use the distance formula, in its various algebraic rearrangements, to solve problems relating to distance, speed, and time.

The unit culminates with a final project in which students bring together all the skills they have mastered. Because the final project is largely of students' own design, it showcases their learning in a very individual and meaningful way.

You can help your child during the unit by discussing how speed, distance, and time are measured, how they relate to one another, and why it is important to understand these quantities in the course of daily living.

Sincerely,

# Reporting Live from the Parade

"This is Monica Chang, from KMTH radio, reporting to you live from our Eye on the Scene hot air balloon. We are hovering above Main Street to give you full coverage of today's parade. I am here with JT Diaz, photographer from the *Times,* and JT's assistant, Latasha Williams, who is here to take notes about each of the photographs. Now, JT, you are taking a lot of pictures," says Monica as she holds her microphone up for JT.

"You bet I am, Monica. It takes 5 seconds for me to take a picture and for Latasha to get down the important details. We have a good, clear view up here," says JT.

"JT is right," says Monica. "The view is wonderful today. We are hovering above Main Street, between Avenue A and Avenue B. There are booths with food and activities all along the way. The parade organizers have spread out the booths so that there is one booth every 15 meters.

"We can see the gas station right on the corner of Main Street and Avenue A. Moving 15 meters down Main Street toward Avenue B, we see the Dog Lover's Club. I hear they're giving away dog treats to anyone with a dog. If you go down the street another 15 meters, you will be at the Taco Zone. Another 15 meters past that is the TreeWatch Group, which is raising money for their environmental work. The next booth, hosted by the *U.F.O. Chronicle,* is giving away copies of its science fiction magazine. The next booth is the popular T-Shirt Hut booth, which is just 15 meters before the stop sign at the corner of Main Street and Avenue B.

"We are currently watching the parade already in progress. JT is taking the first picture, and Latasha is taking notes. On the street below us, I can see the fire-breathing mouth of the dragon float, the drum major from the marching band, and a rollerblader from the Rollerblading Club.

"We'll be back after a word from our sponsors with live coverage of the Main Street Parade. This is Monica Chang."

# Snapshot Sequence Sheet

Avenue B

| | | | | | | | | |
|---|---|---|---|---|---|---|---|---|
| Stop Sign | | | | | | | | |
| T-Shirt Hut | | | | | | | | |
| *U.F.O. Chronicle* | | | | | | | | |
| TreeWatch | | | | | | | | |
| Taco Zone | | | | | | | | |
| Dog Lovers' Club | | | | | | | | |
| Gas Station | | | | | | | | |

Avenue A

**Picture** ___ ___ ___ ___ ___ ___ ___ ___

**Time** ___ ___ ___ ___ ___ ___ ___ ___

# Snapshot Stories

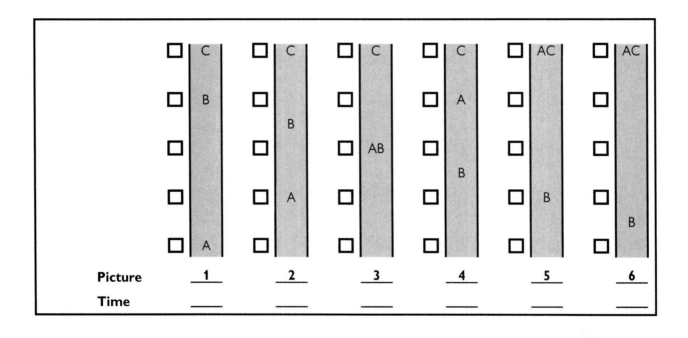

| Picture | 1 | 2 | 3 | 4 | 5 | 6 |
|---------|---|---|---|---|---|---|
| Time | | | | | | |

# Latasha's Field Notes I

## Film Roll 1, Snapshots 1–8

**RB** = Rollerblader, **DM** = Drum Major,
**DF** = Dragon Float

1st Snapshot, 1:00:00 P.M.
    RB: 5 meters past Gas Station
    DM: At Taco Zone
    DF: Stopped at TreeWatch

2nd Snapshot, 1:00:05 P.M.
    RB: At Dog Lovers' Club
    DM: 5 meters past Taco Zone
    DF: Stopped at TreeWatch

3rd Snapshot, 1:00:10 P.M.
    RB: 10 meters past Dog Lovers' Club
    DM: 10 meters past Taco Zone
    DF: Stopped at TreeWatch

4th Snapshot, 1:00:15 P.M.
    RB: 5 meters past Taco Zone
    DM: At TreeWatch
    DF: Stopped at TreeWatch

5th Snapshot, 1:00:20 P.M.
    RB: At TreeWatch
    DM: 5 meters past TreeWatch
    DF: Stopped at TreeWatch

6th Snapshot, 1:00:25 P.M.
    RB: 10 meters past TreeWatch
    DM: 10 meters past TreeWatch
    DF: Stopped at TreeWatch

7th Snapshot, 1:00:30 P.M.
    RB: 5 meters past *U.F.O. Chronicle*
    DM: At *U.F.O. Chronicle*
    DF: Stopped at TreeWatch

8th Snapshot, 1:00:35 P.M.
    RB: At T-Shirt Hut
    DM: 5 meters past *U.F.O Chronicle*
    DF: Stopped at TreeWatch

## Film Roll 1, Snapshots 17–24

**DF** = Dragon Float, **J** = Juggler,
**L** = Lisa

17th Snapshot, 1:01:20 P.M.
    DF: 5 meters past TreeWatch
    J: 10 meters past Dog Lovers' Club
    L: At Gas Station

18th Snapshot, 1:01:25 P.M.
    DF: 10 meters past TreeWatch
    J: 5 meters past Taco Zone
    L: At Dog Lovers' Club

19th Snapshot, 1:01:30 P.M.
    DF: At *U.F.O. Chronicle*
    J: At TreeWatch
    L: At Taco Zone

20th Snapshot, 1:01:35 P.M.
    DF: 5 meters past *U.F.O. Chronicle*
    J: 10 meters past TreeWatch
    L: At TreeWatch

21st Snapshot, 1:01:40 P.M.
    DF: 10 meters past *U.F.O. Chronicle*
    J: 5 meters past *U.F.O. Chronicle*
    L: At *U.F.O. Chronicle*

22nd Snapshot, 1:01:45 P.M.
    DF: At T-Shirt Hut
    J: At T-Shirt Hut
    L: At T-Shirt Hut

23rd Snapshot, 1:01:50 P.M.
    DF: At T-Shirt Hut
    J: At T-Shirt Hut
    L: At T-Shirt Hut

24th Snapshot, 1:01:55 P.M.
    DF: At T-Shirt Hut
    J: At T-Shirt Hut
    L: At T-Shirt Hut

# Latasha's Field Notes II

**Film Roll 2, Snapshots 1–8**

**C** = Clown, **TT** = Tumbling Team, **P** = Pig

Roll 2, 1st Picture, 1:04:00 P.M.

C: At Gas Station

TT: At Dog Lovers' Club

P: At Stop Sign

Roll 2, 2nd Picture, 1:04:05 P.M.

C: At Dog Lovers' Club

TT: 5 meters past Dog Lovers' Club

P: 10 meters from Stop Sign toward T-Shirt Hut

Roll 2, 3rd Picture, 1:04:10 P.M.

C: At Taco Zone

TT: 10 meters past Dog Lovers' Club

P: 5 meters past T-Shirt Hut toward *U.F.O. Chronicle*

Roll 2, 4th Picture, 1:04:15 P.M.

Too cloudy

Roll 2, 5th Picture, 1:04:20 P.M.

Too cloudy

Roll 2, 6th Picture, 1:04:25 P.M.

Too cloudy

Roll 2, 7th Picture, 1:04:30 P.M.

C: At Stop Sign

TT: At TreeWatch

P: At Taco Zone

Roll 2, 8th Picture, 1:04:35 P.M.

Too cloudy

# Steps in Making a Distance-Time Graph

**1.** Begin with the axes for a graph. Label each axis.

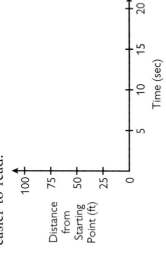

**2.** Set the scale for each axis. Mark equal divisions along each axis to make the graph easier to read.

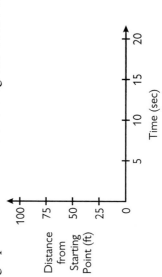

**3.** How long did it take to walk the entire distance? Mark that point.

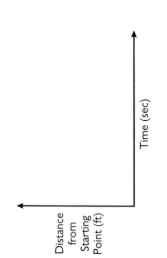

**4.** How long did it take to walk half the distance? Check your data. Mark that point.

**5.** Plot other known data points on the graph.

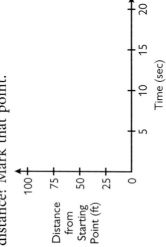

**6.** How can we show the entire walk on the graph? Draw the line showing the entire walk.

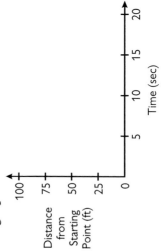

# Centimeter Grid Paper

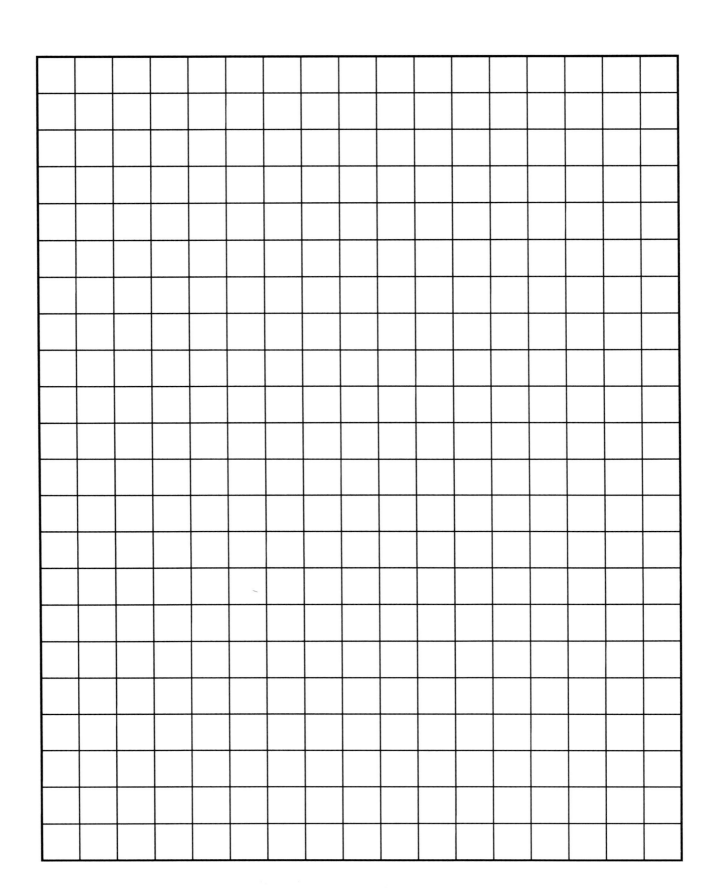

# Stories, Maps, and Graphs: What Was Jessica Doing?

Examine the story, the map, and the graph of Jessica's travels. Use the information provided to answer the following questions. For each question record:

- your answer

- whether your answer is exact or approximate

- whether you used the story, the map, or the graph to find your answer

**a.** How many blocks is it from the grocery store to the school?

**b.** How long did Jessica spend at the grocery store?

**c.** What did she do at the grocery store?

**d.** What time did Jessica meet her friends?

**e.** How long did it take Jessica to get to the grocery store from her house?

**f.** How long did it take Jessica to get back home from the grocery store?

**g.** Why did it take Jessica longer to get home than it did to get to the grocery store?

**h.** How did Jessica get to the store?

**i.** How did she get to the park?

**j.** In what direction was Jessica traveling when she went from her home to the school?

**k.** During what time periods was Jessica staying at one place?

**l.** During what time periods was Jessica traveling farther away from her house?

**m.** During what time periods was Jessica traveling closer to her house?

**n.** When was Jessica traveling the slowest? the fastest?

**o.** Which is closer to Jessica's house, the park or the grocery store?

# Race Graphs

### The Running Race

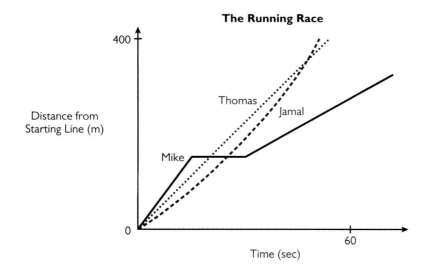

Distance from Starting Line (m)

Thomas

Jamal

Mike

Time (sec)

60

400

### The Swimming Race

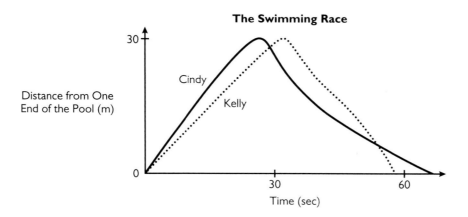

Distance from One End of the Pool (m)

Cindy

Kelly

30

30

60

Time (sec)

### The Three-Legged Race

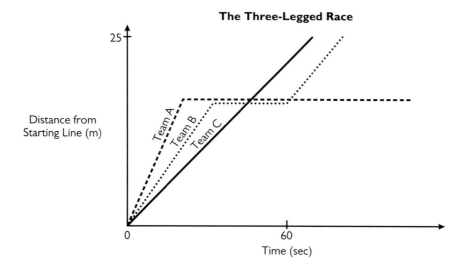

Distance from Starting Line (m)

Team A

Team B

Team C

25

60

Time (sec)

# Distance, Speed, and Time Problems

Solve each of the following problems using the following equations. Then create a graph that you can use to check and show that your answer is correct. Be careful; some of these problems are tricky!

$d = s \times t$ (total distance = average speed × total time)

$s = d \div t$ (average speed = total distance ÷ total time)

$t = d \div s$ (total time = total distance ÷ average speed)

## 1. What is the average speed?

We drove 60 miles to visit our friends' new baby. Then we drove 60 miles to get back home. On the way there, we drove at a speed of 60 miles per hour. On the way back, we drove at a speed of 30 miles per hour. What was our average speed for the whole trip?

## 2. Who won the race?

In a bicycle race of 10 miles, Rachel gave Simone a head start of 2 miles. Simone rode at an average speed of 20 miles per hour. Rachel rode at an average speed of 25 miles per hour. Who won the race?

## 3. Click and Clack's trip

Click and Clack took a trip. The table below shows how long they traveled at each speed.

**a.** How far did they travel during the whole trip?

**b.** How far did they travel at each speed?

**c.** What was their average speed for the trip?

| They Traveled at This Speed | For This Amount of Time |
|---|---|
| 10 kilometers per hour | 10 minutes |
| 20 kilometers per hour | 20 minutes |
| 30 kilometers per hour | 30 minutes |
| 40 kilometers per hour | 40 minutes |

# INDEX

Red type denotes items that appear only in the Teacher's Guide.

equations, slopes, and y-intercepts, 282–283, 306, 287
estimated and measured distances, 52–53
of forecasting techniques, 138–139
using goodness of fit, 155, 158–161, 173
of graphs of exponential functions, 297, 311, 294
of growth models, 145, 158–165, 169, 174–177
of growth predictions, 154–155, 173
of growth spirals, 142–143, 168
using linear equations, 208–209, 221
using mean, median, mode, and range, 8–9, 35
measurements and Pythagorean Theorem calculations, 238–239
population growth, growth rate, and density, 163
prism and pyramid volumes, 115, 130, 112
quadratic equations and their graphs, 290–291, 309, 269H, 286–287
quadratic and linear relationships, 288–289, 308, 286
using a rating scale, 6–7, 34
using scatter plots, 18–19, 39
simple and compound interest, 167
slope estimates and measurements, 227, 228, 256, 257
of stairway slopes, 242–243, 262
using stem-and-leaf plots, 12–13, 37
surface area and volume, 98–99, 120–121, 124, 133, 93
using tree diagrams, 29

**Compound interest,** 167

**Concert tour**
event probabilities and combinations, 26–27, 33
performance order permutations, 30–33, 44
selection tree diagram, 28–29

**Concert Tour Game,** 26–27, 33

**Cone,** 116–117, 131
cross sections, 116, 131, 113
surface area formula, 131, 113

**Conic sections,** 116, 131, 113

**Continuous function,** 156

**Coordinates in a sequence,** 54–55, 80

**Correlations,** types of, 20–21, 40, 15

**Cross product technique,** 241

**Cross sections**
of a cone, 116, 131, 113
of a cube, 96
of a cylinder, 108–109, 128, 103
of a pyramid, 115, 130, 112
of a sphere, 96, 93
of three-dimensional figures, 96–97, 123, 92–93

**Cube**
cross sections, 96, 92
nets for, 95, 92
volume and surface area, 100–101, 125, 93

**Cylinder**
cross sections, 108–109, 128, 103
net for, 108, 128, 103
volume and surface area, 108–109, 128, 103

## D

**Decimals**
as growth numbers, 140–141, 148–149, 167, 170
growth spirals and, 142–143, 168
for tangent ratios, 251–252, 265, 248

**Density,** population, 163

**Dependent variable,** 14

**Designing**
ramps, 247
roads, 248–255, 265–267
stairs, 244–245, 263
mapping, 270–271

**Diagrams**
growth spirals, 142–143, 168
sequence, 54–57, 80, 81
tree, 28–29, 33, 43, 45

**Direct correlation,** 20–21, 40

**Direct variation,** 274–275, 303, 269G, 271

**Direction**
sequence diagrams and, 56–57, 81
speed and, 72–73, 87

**Discrepancy,** model and actual data, 155, 158–161, 173

**Discrete function,** 156

**Distance.** See also Distance-time graphs
calculating, 52–55, 79, 80, 48
estimating, 52–53, 79, 48
measuring, 52–53, 79, 48
time, speed relationship, 52–55, 70–71, 74–75, 79–80, 48

**Distance-time graphs,** 58–67, 82–85, 49, 59
comparing to speed time graphs, 69
interpreting, 66–67, 70–71, 85, 86
making, 60–61, 70–71, 82, 86
types of, 64–65, 83

**Distributive property,** 197, 198–199, 216, 217

**Double bar graph,** interpreting, 7

## E

**Equations.** See also Expressions; Formulas
checking solutions for, 205, 219
of the form $y = ax$, 296–297, 311
of the form $y = k/x$, 276–277, 304
of the form $y = kx$, 274–275, 303, 271
of the form $y = ax^2$, 290–291, 309, 286
integer, 192–193, 214
linear, 204–209, 219–221, 200, 279
for lines between points, 284–285, 307, 279
making comparisons with, 208–209
modeling, 202–207, 218–220, 200
of motion, 55, 74–75, 80, 88

polynomial operations, 202–203, 218
proportions and, 244–245, 263, 241
Pythagorean Theorem, 237, 260, 223G
slope and, 280–283, 305, 306, 279
y-intercept and, 282–283, 306, 279

**Estimation.** See also Prediction
average speed, 72–73
distance, 52–53, 79
using graphs of sequences, 154–155, 173
using growth models, 144–145, 158–165, 169, 174–177
by interpolating an intermediate value, 151, 171
using line of best fit, 22–23, 41
metric length, 16
using patterns, 140–141, 166
slope, 227, 228, 242, 256, 257
speed, 50–51, 54–57, 78, 80, 81
surface area, 99, 124
visual, 16, 22–23, 41, 99, 154–155, 173, 227, 228, 242, 256, 257
volume, 99, 119, 124, 132

**Experimental probability,** 26, 42, 24

**Exponential expressions,** 298–299, 312, 294–295

**Exponential functions,** 294–301, 311–313
definition, 297, 294–295

**Exponential growth**
algebraic description of, 148–149, 151, 170, 171, 294
graphing, 152–155, 158–161, 172–174, 294–295
interpolating intermediate values, 150–151, 154–155, 171, 173
modeling, 158–165, 174–177
patterns, 140–141, 167
predicting with, 144–145, 158–165, 169, 174–177
spiral models of, 142–143, 168

**Exponential regression,** 135H

**Exponents,** 194–301, 311–313
laws of, 298–299, 312, 295

negative, 299, 312
scientific notation and, 300–301,
    313, 269H

**Expressions.** *See also* Equations,
181–189, 210–213, 180, 190
Polynomials
    checking, 199
    combining like terms, 182–183,
        210
    distributive property, 197,
        198–199, 216, 217
    equivalent, 179G, 179H
    evaluating, 184–185, 196–197,
        211
    exponential, 298–299, 312,
        294–295
    for geometric patterns,
        198–199, 217
    grouping symbols and, 196–197,
        216, 180
    for growth sequences, 148–149,
        170
    integer, 192–193, 214
    modeling, 182–187, 192–197,
        210–212, 214–216, 180, 190
    multiplying, 186–189, 212, 213,
        181
    simplifying, 182–183, 194–195,
        210, 215
    writing, 182–183, 188–189,
        198–199

## F

**Face,** of a three-dimensional
    figure, 95

**Factorials,** 32, 25

**Fibonacci sequence,** 168

**Forecasting.** *See* Prediction

**Formulas**
    distance, 55, 74–75, 80, 88, 48
    probability, 26
    surface area of a cone, 131
    surface area of a cube, 124
    surface area of a cylinder, 128,
        103
    surface area of a pyramid, 130,
        112
    surface area of a rectangular
        prism, 126
    volume of a cone, 117, 131,
        113

volume of a cylinder, 109, 103
volume of a prism, 107, 127, 102
volume of a pyramid, 125, 112
volume of a rectangular prism,
    105, 126, 102

**Functions.** *See also* Formulas
    algebraic representation of,
        148–151, 170, 171
    comparing, 140–145,
        166–167
    definition, 273, 270
    direct variation, 274–275, 303,
        269G, 271
    exponential, 294–301, 311–313,
        294–295
    graphing, 152–155, 172–173
    input/output relationships,
        184–185, 211, 270
    input/output rules, 272–273,
        302, 270
    inverse variation, 276–277,
        304
    linear, 278–285, 305–307
    mapping diagrams, 270–271
    modeling, 158–165, 174–177
    quadratic, 286–293, 308–310,
        286–287
    tangent, 250–251, 265
    vertical line test, 271

**Fundamental Counting**
    **Principle,** 29, 24–25

## G

**Galilei, Galileo,** 109

**Generalizations**
    angle relationships in right
        triangles, 234–235, 259
    laws of exponents, 298–299,
        312, 295
    Pythagorean Theorem,
        236–237, 260, 232
    relationship among right
        triangle sides, 236–237, 260
    tangent ratio, 250–251, 265,
        248–249

**Geometric mean,** 173

**Geometric patterns,** algebraic
    expressions for, 198–199, 217

**Geometry.** *See also* Measurement
    angle of elevation, 230–231, 258

classification of prisms,
    104–105, 126
classification of pyramids,
    114–115, 130
classification of three-
    dimensional figures, 94–95,
    122
cone, 116–117, 131, 113
conic sections, 116, 131, 113
cross sections, 96–97, 108–109,
    116, 123, 128, 130, 131,
    92–93
cylinder, 108–109, 128
growth spirals, 142–143, 168
nets, 94–95, 104, 114–115, 122,
    126, 92
prism, 104–107, 126, 127, 102
pyramid, 114–115, 130, 112
Pythagorean Theorem,
    236–239, 260, 261, 223G
Pythagorean triples, 237, 260,
    223G
rectangular prism, 104–105,
    126, 102
right triangle relationships,
    232–239, 259–261, 223G
symmetry, 290
two-dimensional drawings and
    three-dimensional models,
    252–255, 266, 267

**Grade.** *See* Percent grade

**Graph slope**
    for direct variation, 275, 303,
        269G
    distance-time, 60–61, 82, 49, 58
    finding line, 280–281, 305, 280
    for inverse variation, 277, 304
    positive, negative, zero,
        280–281, 305
    relationship to a linear
        equation, 282–283, 306,
        278–279
    sequence diagrams and, 54–55,
        80
    speed-time, 72–73, 87

**Graphing.** *See also* Modeling
    change over time, 62–63,
        70–75, 86–88
    direct variation functions,
        274–275, 303, 269G
    exponential functions, 296–299,
        311, 294–295
    growth sequences, 152–153,
        172, 156

inverse variation functions,
    276–277, 304
line of best fit, 21, 40, 3H
linear functions, 280–285,
    305–307
maximum surface area, 101
motion, 58–67, 72–73, 82–85, 87
population growth, 154–155,
    160–161
quadratic functions, 288–293,
    308–310, 269H, 286–287
sales growth, 158–159, 174

**Graphing calculator,** 3G, 3H,
47G, 135G, 135H, 179H, 223G,
269G, 269H

**Graphs.** *See also* Models
    bar, 7
    circle, 7, 34
    distance-time, 58–67, 82–85, 49,
        59
    double bar, 7
    identifying functions from,
        272–273, 302, 271
    linear, 278–285, 305–307, 271
    scatter plot, 18–23, 39–41,
        152–155, 158–161, 172, 3H, 14
    sequence diagrams and, 54–57,
        80, 81
    speed-time, 72–73, 87, 68

**Grouping symbols,** 196–197, 216

**Growth model,** 156–165, 174–177

**Growth rate,** 162–163, 176

**Growth sequences**
    algebraic description of,
        148–149, 151, 170, 171
    comparing addition and
        multiplication, 140–141, 167,
        135G, 136
    comparing models to data, 155,
        173
    finding the *n*-th term of, 147, 156
    graphing, 152–155, 172, 173
    interpolating intermediate
        values, 150–151, 154–155,
        171, 173
    modeling with, 158–165,
        174–177
    predicting with, 144–145,
        154–155, 158–165, 169,
        173–177
    spirals for, 142–143, 168
    spreadsheet display of, 135G

**Guess-and-check,** for finding growth numbers, 140–141, 144–145, 150, 167, 169, 137

## H

**Height**
of a cone, 116
of a pyramid, 114

**Hill**
three-dimensional model of, 252–253
three-dimensional scale-model of, 254–255, 267

**Homework,** 34–45, 78–89, 122–133, 166–177, 210–221, 256–267, 302–313

**Hypotenuse,** of a right triangle, 239, 232

## I

**Independent variable,** 14

**Indirect measurement**
using proportion, 247, 264
using the Pythagorean Theorem, 238–241, 261, 262
using tangent, 250–251, 265

**Integers.** See also Negative numbers
adding, 192–193, 214
on the coordinate plane, 277, 281
as exponents, 300–301, 313
subtracting, 192–193, 214

**Inverse correlation,** 20–21, 40

**Inverse operations**
addition and subtraction, 144–145, 169
multiplication and division, 144–145, 169
square and square root, 150–151, 171

**Inverse tangent,** 249

**Inverse variation,** 276–277, 304

**Irrational numbers,** 238–239, 261

## L

**Lab Gear**
adding and subtracting integers, 192–193, 214, 191
evaluating expressions, 184–185, 211
evaluating expressions with parentheses, 196–197, 180
multiplying expressions, 186–187, 212, 181
representing expressions, 182–183, 210, 180, 190
simplifying polynomials, 194–195, 215
solving linear equations, 204–207, 219, 220, 200

**Leg,** of a right triangle, 239, 232

**Like terms**
combining, 182–183, 210
combining to simplify expressions, 202–203, 218

**Line of best fit,** 21, 40
finding, 3H
graphing, 3H
making predictions with 22–23, 41

**Line of sight,** 231

**Line of symmetry,** 290

**Linear equations,** 204–209, 219–221, 278–285, 305–307
of the form $y = k/x$, 276–277, 304
of the form $y = kx$, 274–275, 303, 269G, 271
for lines between points, 284–285, 307, 279
modeling, 204–207, 219, 220
slope and, 280–283, 305, 306, 279
solving, 204–209, 219–221, 200
y-intercept and, 282–283, 306, 279

**Linear functions,** 278–285, 305–307

**Linear graph**
slope and, 280–283, 305, 306, 279
writing an equation for, 284–285, 307, 279

y-intercept and, 282–283, 306, 279

**Linear growth**
algebraic description of, 148–149, 151, 170, 171
graphing, 152–155, 158–161, 172–174
interpolating intermediate values, 150–151, 154–155, 171, 173
modeling, 158–165, 174–177
patterns, 140–141, 167
predicting with, 144–145, 154–155, 158–165, 169, 173–177
spiral models of, 142–143, 168

**Linear regression,** 3H, 135H

**Lists,** using a graphing calculator to work with, 3G

**Logic.** See also Number sense, Patterns; Sequences
converse, 233
following clues, 10
if-then form, 233
impossible graphs, 67, 85
inconsistent statements, 85
making a data-based argument, 8–9, 35
making generalizations, 234–237, 250–251, 259, 260, 265
number trick analysis, 188–189, 213
proof using expressions, 188–189, 213
recognizing enough information, 70–71
relative location, 70–71, 86
relative speed, 54–55, 80
statements, 233
tree diagrams, 28–29, 33, 43, 45
working backward, 10–11, 36

## M

**Map,** distance, 62–63, 83

**Mapping diagrams,** 270–271

**Math Background,** 4–5, 14–15, 24–25, 48–49, 58–59, 68–69, 92–93, 102–103, 112–113, 136–137, 146–147, 156–157, 180–181, 190–191, 200–201, 224–225, 232–233, 240–241, 248–249, 270–271, 278–279, 286–287, 294–295

**Mathematical forecasting.** See Prediction

**MathScape Online,** 3, 3G, 3H, 47, 47G, 47H, 91, 91G, 91H, 135, 135H, 179, 179G, 179H, 223, 223H, 269, 269H

**MathScape Online Self-Check Quizzes,** 5, 15, 25, 49, 59, 69, 93, 103, 113, 137, 147, 157, 181, 191, 201, 225, 233, 241, 249, 271, 279, 287, 295

**Maximum surface area,** 100–101, 125

**Mean**
affect of changing data values on, 3G
for analyzing athletic performance, 8–9, 35
for analyzing a survey, 6–7, 34
arithmetic, 173
back-to-back stem-and-leaf plot and, 17, 38
geometric, 173
stem-and-leaf plot and, 12–13, 37
using a graphing calculator to find, 3G
working backward to create a data set from, 10–11, 36, 4

**Measurement.** See also Scale
drawing accuracy, 227
angle of elevation, 230–231, 258
area, 288, 292
converting among units of area, 118, 132
converting among units of length, 52–53, 79
converting among units of time, 52–53, 79
converting among units of volume, 118–119, 132
estimating speed, 50–51, 54–57, 78, 80, 81, 48

estimating, 50–51, 54–57, 72–73, 78, 80, 81, 48
relative, 54–55, 80
sequence diagrams and, 55–57, 80, 81
speed-time graphs, 72–73, 87, 69
time, distance relationship, 52–55, 70–71, 74–75, 48, 68–69
variability, 72–73, 87

**Speed-time graphs,** 72–73, 87, 68
comparing to distance-time graphs, 69

**Sphere,** cross section of, 96, 93

**Spreadsheet,** 135G

**Spirals,** for growth sequences, 142–143, 168

**Square root,** 150–151, 171

**Stairs**
designing, 244–245, 263
slope ratios for, 242–243, 262
stair-building design guidelines, 245

**Statistics.** See also Probability
analysis using a back-to-back stem-and-leaf plot, 16–17, 38
analysis using mean and percent, 6–7, 34
analysis using a scatter plot, 18–23, 39–41
analysis using a stem-and-leaf plot, 12–13, 37
analysis using a systematic list, 27, 42
analysis using a tree diagram, 28–29, 43
correlations, 20–21, 40, 15
line of best fit, 21–23, 40, 41, 3H
outliers, 12–13, 5
ranking using mean, median, mode, and range, 8–9, 35
working backward to create data sets, 10–11, 36

**Stem-and-leaf plot**
back-to-back, 16–17, 38
creating and comparing, 12–13, 37, 5

**Subtraction**
grouping symbols and, 196–197, 216

integer, 192–193, 214
of polynomials, 202–203, 218
for simplifying polynomials, 194–195, 215

**Surface area**
of a compound figure, 111, 129
of a cone, 117, 131
of a cylinder, 108–109, 128, 103
of a cube, 93
estimating, 99, 124
maximum, 100–101, 125
measuring, 98–99, 124
of a nonrectangular prism, 106–107, 127
of a pyramid, 114–115, 130, 112
of a rectangular prism, 104–105, 126, 102
relationship to volume, 98–101, 124, 125, 91G, 91H
of a skyscraper, 120–121, 133

**Survey,** analysis using mean and percent, 6–7, 34

**Symbols,** factorial, 32, 25

**Symmetry,** 290

**Systematic list,** for finding combinations, 27, 42

# T

**Tangent ratio,** 250–251, 265, 248

**Technology**
Calculator-Based-Ranger (CBR), 47G
Graph Action™, 47H
graphing calculator, 3G, 3H, 47G, 135G, 135H, 179H, 223G, 269G, 269H
spreadsheet, 135G
MathScape Online, 3, 3G, 3H, 47, 47G, 47H, 91, 91G, 91H, 135, 135H, 179, 179G, 179H, 223, 223H, 269, 269H

**Term,** of a polynomial, 194

**Tessellation,** 259

**Theorem**
Permutation, 32–33, 45
Pythagorean, 236–239, 260–261, 223G, 232
converse of, 233

**Theoretical probability,** 26–27, 42, 24
combinations and, 27–29, 42, 43
Permutation Theorem and, 32–33, 45
permutations and, 30–31, 44

**Three-dimensional figures**
classification of, 94–95, 122
cones, 116–117, 131, 113
cross sections of, 96–97, 108–109, 116, 123, 128, 130, 131, 92–93
cylinders, 108–109, 128, 103
measuring surface area and volume, 98–99, 124
nets for, 94–95, 108, 114–115, 122, 128, 91G
nonrectangular prisms, 106–107, 127, 102
pyramid and prism hill models, 252–255, 266, 267
pyramids, 114–115, 130, 112
rectangular prisms, 104–105, 126, 102

**Time**
converting among units of, 52–53, 79
distance, speed relationship, 52–55, 70–71, 74–75, 48
distance-time graphs, 58–67, 82–85, 49, 59
estimating, 50–51, 78, 48
speed-time graphs, 72–73, 87, 68

**Tree-diagram,** 28–29, 33, 43, 45, 24
permutations and, 31, 44

**Triangle,** right triangle relationships, 232–239, 259–261, 223G, 232, 248

**Trigonometry**
inverse tangent, 249
right triangle relationships, 232–239, 259–261, 223G, 232
tangent ratio, 250–251, 265, 248

**Two-dimensional figures**
area of compound figures, 110, 129
cross sections of three-dimensional figures, 96–97, 123, 92–93, 112–113
as faces of three-dimensional figures, 94–95, 108, 122

as prism bases, 104–107, 126, 127, 102

# V

**Variables**
algebraic, 182
correlations and, 20–21, 40
dependent, 4
independent, 4
scatter plots and, 18–19, 39

**Vertex (vertices)**
of a cone, 116
of a pyramid, 114
of a three-dimensional figure, 95

**Vertical line test,** 271

**Volume**
of compound figures, 111, 129
of a cone, 117, 131, 113
of a cube, 93
converting among units of, 118–119, 132
of a cylinder, 108–109, 128, 103
estimating, 99, 119, 124, 132
measuring, 98–99, 124
of a nonrectangular prism, 106–107, 127, 102
of a pyramid, 114–115, 130, 112
of a rectangular prism, 104–105, 126, 102
relationship to surface area, 98–101, 124, 125, 91H

# W

**Weak,** positive correlation, 21

**Working backward,** creating data sets, 10–11, 36

# Y

y-intercept, 282–283, 306, 287

# Z

**Zero slope,** 280–281, 305, 240